THE
FOUR FACES
of
CHRIST

GEORGE SHAMBLIN

Many of us could name a once-in-a-lifetime friend. I certainly can. John Abernathy, thank you, my brother in Jesus, for being that guy.

And to Trevor Anderson, the third son I always wanted to have. Let's go and do mighty things for the Kingdom of our God.

A B O U T
T H E   A U T H O R

In the summer of 1995, George Shamblin left a career in pharmaceutical sales to enroll at Reformed Theological Seminary in Jackson, Mississippi.

Since 2012, Shamblin has been a pastor at The Center for Executive Leadership in Birmingham, Alabama, where he teaches Bible Studies and disciples others at various stages of spiritual growth. He served on the board of Reel-Life International and taught as an adjunct professor at Birmingham Theological Seminary. In 2023, he and his brother Keith co-founded a missions ministry to Cuba, The Overseas Initiative.

Shamblin published his first book, The Relay, in 2020, followed by Inerrancy in 2023, and was recently inducted into Marquis Who's Who. An avid outdoorsman and Master Gardener, George and his wife of 32 years, Jill, have four children Sydney, Bailey, Miller, and George Jr.

GEORGESHAMBLIN.COM

C O N T E N T S

PART III
What Do You Want Us To Do?

INTRODUCTION

"What do you see?" my mother gently whispered in her beautiful, long-winded southern drawl, which resembled more of a soft lullaby than an accent. "Not much," I replied, "except for the front yard."

"Now, George, you must look closer. What else do you see?" she continued, using up three syllables rather than one to sound out my name.

"I see our mailbox, a big tree, a squirrel." Evidently, I was missing something right in front of my nose but had no idea what.

The occasion was a tranquil afternoon in the deep south, with little else happening. The sights, sounds, and particularly the smells of my childhood have a pleasant way of bringing peace and calm. As if it were yesterday, I vividly recall how the sun was settling in for the night; its last few rays of splendor fast fading but still shining through the front-door window of our home in Patton Place.

Sensing my apprehensiveness, my mother eased me off to my right, spinning me back a half-circle or so to look where I'd just been standing. From this new vantage point, everything was different. When I stood off to the side, I saw the sun's rays beaming into the front parlor from the west.

Questioning once again, my mother whispered, "Now then, what do you see?" I could make out thousands of shiny dust particles that had been there all along. They'd obviously glistened moments before, but I just couldn't see them. Now, I could. They lit up the entire foyer.

"Remember, Georgie," my mother basked while admiring her point well-made, "There's always more to see...but you must look for it."

Had you lived in the 1st Century, as conflicting as it feels, you could not have picked Jesus out of a crowd. Even if someone pointed Him out, saying, "He's right there," you would have found it hard to believe them. According to Isaiah 53:2, "He has no stately form or majesty that we should look upon Him, nor appearance that we should be attracted to Him."

This stands in stark contrast to murals and paintings depicting Him with wavy brown hair, royal blue eyes, and an inviting demeanor. Some rabbis anticipated the Messiah to be leprous or deformed, influenced by passages like Isaiah 53:3-4: "And like one from whom men hide their face He was despised, and we did not esteem Him. Surely our griefs He Himself bore, and our sorrows He carried; Yet we ourselves esteemed Him stricken, Smitten of God, and afflicted."

In essence, if you were in the presence of Christ 2000 years ago and were asked, "What do you see?", your reply would likely have mirrored my response to my mother: "Not much."

The earliest Christians had no better insight into Christ's appearance than we do today. Surprisingly, the New Testament authors remained largely silent on the subject, providing only a rare reference, mostly in passing. With the exception of sarcastic graffiti, depictions of Jesus were noticeably scarce in the first 200 years of Christianity. In summary, there is not a single historical reference that sheds light on what Jesus looked like during His time on earth.

If you were to encounter Jesus today, you might find His physical appearance less compelling (the scars, perhaps, but aspects like complexion, skin tone, face, eyes, hair, etc., not so much), let alone considering what He has to say. I resonate strongly with Francis Chan's assertion, "*If Jesus were the Pastor of your church, you probably wouldn't go there.*"

I would argue however, that although Matthew, Mark, Luke and John may not explicitly sketch out Jesus' physical appearance, there absolutely is something specific they intend for us to perceive.

In Matthew's analysis, for instance, its inescapable how distinctly Jewish our Lord appears, not by happenstance but by thoughtful design. Matthew shines a spotlight on the Jewishness of Jesus, with Old Testament characterizations scattered throughout.

Mark's intention, on the other hand, is quite different. He aims to introduce Christ to a largely Gentile audience. Considering the familiarity Gentiles had with pantheons of Greek gods, it's not surprising Mark chose "the Son of God" as his favorite designation for Jesus.

Luke, the ultimate outsider who never saw Jesus and the only non-Jewish author in Scripture, skillfully captured Jesus' heart for underdogs who saw themselves on the outside looking in. Not only does Luke emphasize how they, too, have a seat at the Lord's table, it's those who see themselves as "in" who paradoxically get left out.

John's sketch, distinguishable at every turn from the others, diverges significantly at numerous points. Whereas Matthew, Mark, and Luke[1] seem to share a common palate for their portrayals of Christ, John breaks out an altogether new color schematic. His account is accentuated with a divine flare; yes, Jesus is Messiah, Son of God, and Son of Man, but He is every bit equally God. Much more on all of this to come.

4 ARTISANS 1 MASTERPIECE

Why are there four accounts of the same story? Was it absolutely necessary? Had the authors been artisans, let's contemplate in response to those questions. Consider some of the greats from

---

[1]   We refer to Matthew, Mark and Luke as the synoptic Gospels due to their similarities.

the Enlightenment, such as Michelangelo, da Vinci, Titian, and Raphael. What would happen if we commissioned each with the same assignment? "**_Show_** us what you see when you look at Jesus [instead of merely **_telling_** us]." Their respective portrayals would be fantastically unique.

Michelangelo might present us with his *The Last Judgement* arching above the Sistine Chapel's altar. In contrast, his contemporary, the inventive Leonardo da Vinci, might opt for a blueprint or diagram akin to his *Universal Man*. Titian, renowned for vividness and emotional depth, could emphasize the human experience of Jesus, capturing moments of intensity, struggle, and profound emotion. As for Raphael, a bitter rival of Michelangelo, he was known for creating harmonious compositions and graceful figures. His contribution might emphasize the compassionate and merciful aspects of Jesus.

What would art be with only one artist, or music minus all but one musician? Imagine the Louvre without the *Mona Lisa* or Florence without *David*. Consider what the world would have missed if all but one of the Enlightenment greats had remained obscure. Simply put, the four gospels are no different.

4 STREET CORNERS 1 COLLISION

The vantage point also plays a crucial role in all of this. The significance of which Gospel writer saw what and from where cannot be overstated. In art, a vantage point, often referred to as a "station point," is a specific, fixed location—either high (bird's-eye-view) or low (worm's-eye-view)—from which a viewer observes and engages with the depicted subject. It serves as the reference point that influences the viewer's perspective on the entire composition.

To diagram or map this out, envision a bustling four-way intersection where a wreck has occurred. Rather than vehicles crashing into each other, picture grace and truth colliding head-on in the person of Jesus Christ. I've strategically placed Matthew on one street corner, up close and personal as events unfolded. As one of 12 disciples, very little obstructed his view. His recollections are crisp, sharp, and full of intricate details.

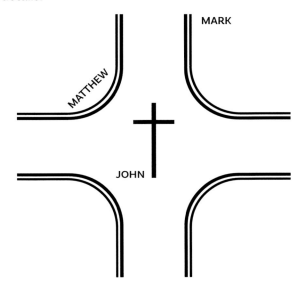

As for Mark, he's positioned halfway down the block. He was close enough in proximity to be an eyewitness but needs assistance nailing down the particulars. There's every reason to believe much of his source material was obtained secondhand from Peter. According to reliable church tradition, it was Mark who fled naked while Christ was on trial: "*A young man was following Him, wearing nothing but a linen sheet over his naked body; and they seized him. But he pulled free of the linen sheet and escaped naked.*"[2] Mark was there, as I like to put it, but not right there.

What about Luke? Where was he? Luke was nowhere to be found in the immediate aftermath of events. He resembled an investigator who later shows up to a crime scene to obtain as much eyewitness testimony as possible. Luke never physically heard or saw Jesus but

---

[2] Mark 14:51-52

interviewed others who did prior to submitting his final report to a Roman official named Theophilus. How do we know that? He tells us:

> **Luke 1:1-4:** _1Since many have undertaken to compile an account of the things accomplished among us, 2just as they were handed down to us by those who from the beginning were eyewitnesses and servants of the word, 3it seemed fitting to me as well, having investigated everything carefully from the beginning, to write it out for you in an orderly sequence, most excellent Theophilus; 4so that you may know the exact truth about the things you have been taught._

Furthermore, how else could Luke have known things like what Mary was pondering in her heart unless she was the one who told him?

As for John, he was not only a member of Jesus' inner circle of three, but, by his own reckoning, appeared as close to Christ as anyone. Self-described as the one whom Jesus loved, it was he who leaned against the breast of Christ during the Passover meal. For that reason, I've placed Him closer to the wreckage than any other, right in the middle of the intersection.

Between the four, it's as if one by one, Matthew, Mark, Luke and John ease the reader off to a street corner and pose a question similar to that of my mother: "Now then, what do you see?" And just when you think you've read it all a million times before, a new gem of gospel-truth emerges to the fore, not dissimilar to fine particles of gold waiting to be found.

And just when you think you've read it all a million times before, a new gem of gospel-truth emerges to the fore, not dissimilar to fine particles of gold waiting to be found.

WHERE FAITH BECOMES SIGHT & PRAYERS BECOME PRAISE

On Monday, November 1st, the Holy Spirit prodded me to visit my sweet mother in the ICU before leading my early morning men's group. She had been non-communicative for the last month. What unfolded during that visit could very well be the most profound moment of my entire life. In fact, it was. My dear mother stood at the threshold between this life and that. Despite conditions improving one day and taking a turn for the worse the next, we never doubted what was next. Our certainty lay in an incident six weeks prior when she incessantly inquired, "Whose voice keeps calling my name? Who is that?" to an empty room. From that point forward, we lent 100x more credence to that Person's voice than any lab result or medical personnel.

I hadn't prepared any last words to tell her if given the chance; for all intents and purposes, she was already gone. Sometimes, the Holy Spirit gently nudges you so. Rounding the corner, gently peeling back the curtain, never in a million years could I anticipate her eyes locking with mine. This wasn't a glazed look, nor was she peering through me like glass. It was a gaze that resonated, that connected. Breaking out, unrehearsed and from the hip, I exclaimed "Sandra, I can't wait to see you again at the last resurrection, okay? We will meet each other again then, okay?" I was awestruck seeing her head nodding in hearty, though incredibly frail, agreement.

I certainly don't believe in luck; but as I left, I felt ecstatic, exclaiming over and over again to myself, "I'm the luckiest person in the world! Wow. I'm the luckiest person in the world!"

Later that evening, among family members packing out the ICU room, we joined together to sing the Doxology. In a fitting and almost poetic manner, the nurse slipped in to tell us, "The exact second you ended with 'Amen,' her heart monitor went flat."

Oh, how marvelously the tables do turn. Reminiscent of childhood memories (that death has a way of resurfacing), it brought me back to that same picturesque moment in Patton Place. And how the sun was settling in for the night. And how my mother spun me around to look where I'd just been standing. A new vantagepoint arose from which everything appeared different. Similar to heaven where faith becomes sight and prayers become praise.

"Now then," I was wont to ask my mom, "Please tell me. What do you see?" Had she been able to answer, "Unspeakable" I'd guess her reply, echoing softly in her beautiful, long-winded southern drawl.

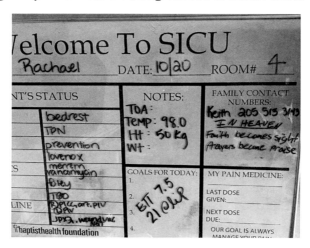

Until we reach heaven or experience His return to earth, whichever comes first, here's what we do have: four separate paintings of the same Savior and His message, each presented by four different men. As we navigate through each of these "faces" depicted, we begin to perceive the King of Creation in a much clearer light. It's akin to observing the back of a tapestry where we can make out bits and pieces, but our conception is capped until the finished product gets flipped around. Stated perfectly, "For now we see in a mirror dimly, but then face to face; now I know in part, but then I will know fully just as I also have been fully known." (1st Cor. 13:12)

Regardless of what Jesus looks like, I truly believe we will be awestricken when engulfed by His presence. Unbridled love. Unfiltered. Welcome to the Four Faces of Christ.

Discussion Questions for Intro: What Do You See?

Exploring Jesus' Appearance:

1. Discuss the contrast between popular depictions of Jesus and the biblical description provided in Isaiah 53:2. How does this challenge our preconceived notions?

2. Why do you think the New Testament authors were largely silent on Jesus' physical appearance? What significance does this hold for believers?

Purpose of Four Gospels:

3. Consider the analogy of commissioning four artists to depict Jesus. How does this illustrate the uniqueness and diversity of the gospel narratives?

Vantage Point and Gospel Writers:

4. Using the intersection visual, compare the perspectives of Matthew, Mark, Luke, and John as described in the text. Talk through how each writer's background and proximity to Jesus influence their portrayal.

5. How does understanding the different vantage points of the gospel writers enhance our appreciation of the gospel narratives?

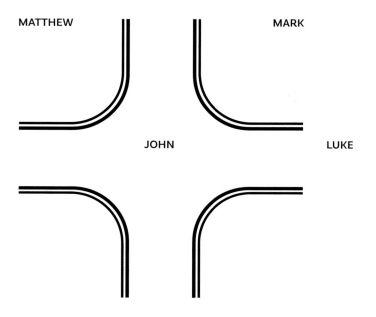

Personal Reflection:

6. In what ways would you agree with Francis Chan, "*If Jesus were the Pastor of your church, you probably wouldn't go there.*"

7. Reflect on a moment in your life where your understanding of Jesus deepened or shifted. What factors contributed to this change?

8. Consider the author's experience with his mother's passing and the connection to seeing Jesus clearly in the afterlife. How does this inspire your own perspective on eternity and encountering Jesus?

9. Have you found this quote to be true, and if so, how? *And just when you think you've read it all a million times before, a new gem of gospel-truth emerges to the fore, not dissimilar to fine particles of gold waiting to be found.*

Action Step for Next Week:

If you could get answers to *any* three questions from God what would they be? In essence, if the tapestry were flipped. Write questions here:

a)

b)

c)

PART 1

What Do You See?

The Rosetta Stone

CHAPTER 1

Matthew, What Do You See?

"I See a Wonderful, Marvelous Savior, Redeemer and Friend"

For centuries, archeologists grappled with the mysteries of ancient hieroglyphics, often left to mere speculation regarding their meaning. One day, they uncovered a dark "Rosetta Stone" that rendered the same text in Greek and Egyptian script and previously undecipherable hieroglyphics. By comparing the translations side by side, they mastered hieroglyphics and could now see clearly into a world they had known only in a fog.

More than any other book in Scripture, Matthew's Gospel is a type of "Rosetta Stone" when making sense of the Old Testament. It's as if the oracles of ancient saints and sages past (i.e., the Torah), who had plenty of strange and foreign concepts akin to hieroglyphics of their own, become ever discernable under Matthew's guidance. When the book of Matthew is placed next to Isaiah, for example, one dispels darkness in the other. Hues of hazy grey in Isaiah, Matthew casts in brisk color. Clarity, in essence, gets cast on confusion.

What could centuries of Hebrew students and rabbis make of a young virgin birthing a Child? Such has never occurred in the history of man. And not just any Child, we're told, but an Infant who Himself was very God of very God. Jews, remember, were emphatically monotheistic. Isaiah 7:14, written 700 hundred years in advance of Christ's birth, predicted, "Behold, a virgin will be with Child and bear a Son, and she will call His name Immanuel." That is to say the baby would be Elohim, which is the designation reserved for Israel's God!

Even had Israel's educated elite dismissed Isaiah 7:14 out of hand, equally perplexing texts followed closely on its heels. A few chapters later, Isaiah continues by saying, "A Child will be born to us, a Son will be given to us; And the government will rest on His shoulders; And His Name will be called Wonderful Counselor, Mighty **God**, Eternal **Father**, Prince of Peace."[3] It's hard to fathom how terribly confusing it must have been for monotheistic Jews to conceive of calling a little Child "Mighty God" or "Eternal Father." The statement, "Ten thousand times in history a baby has become a King. But only once in history has a King become a baby" may be evident now but not back then.

It wasn't as if this peculiar Child King would grow up to enjoy a trouble-free, blissful life, far from it. As bizarre as it sounded, God's predetermined plan appeared to have Him travel down a pathway marked by striking irony. As Supreme Leader over all creation, He would be tried, judged, and declared guilty by a lesser tribunal, one Pontius Pilate. And for some troublesome reason, this same Godlike figure would find Himself on the bitter, brutal receiving end of beatings, leaving scars and stripes across His back, hairs on His beard ripped off, naked, alone, and afraid.[4]

Please be aware that we, as followers of Christ, have the express benefit of *looking back* at the Old Testament through the lens of the cross. Not so for millennia of individuals who stood on the opposite

---

[3] Isaiah 9:6
[4] Not "fear" in the sense we as humans fear, but more of a holy dread of what would transpire soon.

side of Christ's cross. We cannot minimize the fog that clouded their perception of difficult-to-understand passages like those that follow.

a) When Christians read, "He was pierced through for our transgressions...by His stripes, we are healed" (Is. 53:5), we see a depiction of Jesus' hands pierced to the cross and scourge marks striped across His back. But the Jews in Isaiah's day didn't; the earliest record of crucifixion dates to 519 BC, when King Darius I of Persia crucified 30,000 of his political enemies.

b) When we meditate on "He was oppressed, and He was afflicted, Yet *He did not open His mouth; * Like a lamb that is led to slaughter, and like a sheep that is silent before its shearers, so *He did not open His mouth*" (Is. 53:7), it's easy to make the connection to John the Baptist's declaration from the Jordan's riverbanks—"Behold! The Lamb of God who takes away the sin of the world!"[5] In addition, there's "the sudden withdrawal of red letters" for every step Christ takes closer to the hill He would die on—Calvary. If you can access a Bible with Christ's words in red, open it to see for yourself.[6] Chapter 25 is entirely red; 100% of the content has Jesus talking. Then, in Chapter 26, the red begins fading off the page. By Chapter 27, there are less than a dozen red words—a direct fulfillment of Isaiah's prophecy: "Like a sheep that is silent before its shearers, so *He did not open His mouth*." This is just one of 47 prophecies in Isaiah fulfilled by Christ.[7]

c) Or what about the time Isaiah predicted, "His appearance was marred more than any man. And His form more than the sons of men" and "like one from whom men hide their faces,"[8] It's not hard for us to envision the aftereffects of

---

[5]   John 1:29
[6]   NIV, ESV, NKJV, NLT
[7]   https://www.gotquestions.org/prophecies-of-Jesus.html
[8]   Isaiah 52:14; 53:3

Christ's beating by a cat of nine tails. In respect to the jeering crowds who turned away their heads in disgust? Christians are fully aware of how horrid crucifixion was, so how could the citizenry not? As for pockets of Hebrew scholars who studied the exact same text above? *They conjectured the Messiah would be leprous!* It's a plausible deduction if you go back and reread it.

How on earth could any of God's chosen people possibly understand any of these predictions, more akin to undecipherable Egyptian hieroglyphics? Enter on the scene a tax-collecting traitor turned disciple named Matthew.

JESUS' DNA

If Messianic fingerprints were traced throughout the Old Testament from Matthew's vantage point, no verse would be free of Jesus' DNA. His imprint is everywhere; it's inescapable. Like an investigator at a crime scene, Matthew lifts Jesus' fingerprints, comings and goings, footprints, timelines, time stamps, and dates as clear as day. He quoted the Old Testament more than any other writer (61 times). Look for yourself to see how prevalent the word "fulfilled" is.

Right out of the chute, beginning in chapter one, verse one, could any more extraordinary and iconic heroes from the Old Testament be tied to Jesus than Abraham and David: "The record of the genealogy of Jesus the Messiah, the Son of David, the Son of Abraham." (Matthew 1:1) By immediately tying Christ to father Abraham, there's no mistaking how Matthew interpreted the declaration given to Abraham by God in Genesis 12:3, "In you all the families of the earth will be blessed." Abraham smiled at the Lord's promise of blessing all nations (goyim in Hebrew) through one of his offspring. As for the tie to King David and the final occupant of his throne, that seat was exclusively reserved for King Jesus. "Are you the King of the Jews?" Pilate asked, to which Jesus confirmed, "It is as you say."[9]

We must acknowledge two additional giants of the faith who later emerge in Matthew. While on the Mount of Transfiguration we overhear Moses, symbolizing the Law, and Elijah, representing the Prophets, deliberate with Christ about the forthcoming events in Jerusalem. Not surprisingly, Jesus said earlier, "Do not think that I came to abolish the Law or the Prophets; I did not come to abolish but to fulfill." How fascinating to learn only in the person of Christ can one individual simultaneously hold the three highest offices in Judaism: Prophet, Priest, and King. Matthew covered two of those offices here, Law and Prophet, and was just getting started.[10]

The easiest way to summarize his 28 remaining chapters is that Matthew, in essence, was a Jew writing to Jews about a Jew, meaning he locked down on the Jewishness of Jesus, or what one professor deemed "a distinctly Jewish flavor" throughout. This allowed him to realize the long-awaited "Anointed One" or "Messiah" had finally come. As opposed to Mark, who usually refers to Jesus as the Son of God, which connects more to his Gentile audience. Or Luke, who refers to Jesus primarily as the Son of Man for his purposes. Or John, who saw Jesus as God.

By the way, you've got a head start going into this next section, because, you'll be surprised to learn, you're already familiar with the Hebrew word for *Anointed One* and the Greek word for *Anointed One*. I guarantee it, although you might not have put two and two together. Give it your best guess before looking up the answer in the footnotes.[11]

---

[9] Matthew 17:11
[10] Hebrews 6:20 describes Jesus as High Priest this way: "Where Jesus has entered as a forerunner for us, having become a high priest forever according to the order of Melchizedek."
[11] The Old Testament was written in the Hebrew language and the Hebrew word for *Anointed One* is Messiah. The New Testament was written in the Greek language. The Greek word for *Anointed One* is Christ. We refer to Jesus as the Messiah or Jesus Christ. Neither is His last Name but designates He's the One.

AFTERIMAGE

What about the Torah's interconnection with Jesus? What was Matthew to make of that? Time had been on his side, meaning he had decades to flesh out what that interconnection looked like.[12] I can envision Matthew staring at Jesus stacked up against the Torah until he stared his eyes away. Until, in the final analysis, he bursts out, "I see it!" The best way to illustrate that is by using the optical illusion below.

Focus on the 4 dots in the middle for 30 seconds. Then take a look at smooth single color wall (preferably white) and you should see a circle of light. Blink your eyes a few times and you will see Jesus.

The rabbis saw what you saw at first glance...bits and pieces in anticipation of the Coming One. But after locking in on the image for 30 seconds, then turning to a solid surface, "I see it!", you saw Jesus. That's precisely what happened with Matthew.

When arranging his material, one overarching theme between the Old and New Testaments was perceived: Jesus = Torah and Torah = Jesus.

---

[12] It's estimated an interval of 30-40 years transpired between Jesus' ascension (c. 29 AD) and the publication of Matthew's Gospel.

How do we know this? I can only think of one thing all sects of Jews could reach a consensus on—they all agreed the *Five Books* of Moses were authoritative (the TORAH). Differences arose over the authority of other books like the Prophets, Writings, Talmud, Mishnah, etc., In light of that insight (i.e., all Jews agreeing on the Torah's validity), Matthew intentionally broke up his account into *five teaching blocks* (each block ends with "when Jesus had finished teaching...").[13] By design, Matthew was reinforcing how our Lord fulfilled "every jot and tittle" of the Law. I assure you that his fivefold division did not go unnoticed by his Hebrew readership. Not to mention a blatant reference in chapter 5: "Do not think that I came to abolish the Law or the Prophets; I did not come to abolish but to fulfill."

Furthermore, when deciding on how many sermons and discourses to recount, Matthew could have picked any number he wanted, correct? Yes, he intentionally chose five, beginning with the Sermon on the Mount. Once again, Jesus = Torah and Torah = Jesus.

THE DOOR YOU REACH

The long and winding road
That leads to your door
Will never disappear
I've seen that road before
It always leads me here
Lead me to your door

– The Beatles

Whenever I read the Gospel according to Matthew, I'm reminded of the Beatles' hit song, "The Long and Winding Road." In 1968, Paul McCartney said about its release: "It's a sad song because it's all

---

[13] Matthew 7:28; 11:1; 13:53; 19:1; 26:1

about the unattainable, the door you never quite reach. This is the road you never get to the end of."[14]

It's as if McCartney's sentiments about *the unattainable, the door you never quite reach, the road you never get to the end of,* all speak for what the ancient saints and sages past must have experienced collectively, which was a sense of hopelessness trying to figure out how all the pieces of a 1,500-year-old puzzle fit together.[15] Not so for Matthew.

I'll never forget a memorable lesson I learned from my son Miller in the backyard of our house in Pensacola. He insisted, all 30 inches tall of his three-year-old frame, that my missing gardening hand shovel was lying in the middle of a path in the woods. Taking him at his word, I paced back and forth all over the area he designated, seeking to find the entrance without any luck. "There!" he motioned, flinging his arm while standing on the back deck. I walked a little to my right. "Not there. There!" he pointed again, his slight kid lisp revving with agitation, causing me to chuckle. A grin, by the way, I shielded with my shoulder, not wanting to exasperate what he interpreted as a dire situation. (If only adult life were that simple.)

Nevertheless, I obliged by taking a few steps to the left. "There!" again and again we went. Finally, that little tyke came bee-bopping down the patio stairs, like a grumpy, grouchy old-timer, to point out what I could not see. "There!" he squatted down with the front of his head practically touching the ground, his pointer finger extended within inches of the two-and-a-half-foot tall "entrance" to the path where my missing hand shovel lay. And he was right; the opening had been there the entire time, all thirty inches high of it; I just kept missing it.

In answer to the question, "Matthew, what did you see?", I'm reminded of that life lesson I learned from a child twenty-some years ago.

---

[14] Miles, Barry. *Paul McCartney: Many Years from Now.*
[15] The Bible is a collection of 66 books written by more than 40 authors over a period of about 1,500 years.

Matthew beheld what the whole world had missed, what they had walked past, and what they had known for centuries only in a fog: Jesus of Nazareth was the long-awaited Christ. That's what he saw.

Discussion Questions for "Matthew, What Do You See?"

Look Back:

Share your three questions from last week and why you chose each.

Understanding the Rosetta Stone Analogy:

1. How does the analogy of the Rosetta Stone help us understand the relationship between the Old Testament and the New Testament?

2. Using the stem and leaf plot, classify in the Old Testament where prophecies or themes are clarified or fulfilled in the Gospel of Matthew. An example has been provided for you.

OLD TESTMENT	MATTHEW
Is. 53:7	Chap. 17

Matthew's Unique Perspective:

3. Explore Matthew's background as a tax-collecting disciple and his role in presenting Jesus as the fulfillment of Old Testament prophecy. How does Matthew's perspective contribute to our understanding of Jesus' mission?

4. When reading Matthew's genealogy in the opening verses of his Gospel, what significance does linking Jesus to Abraham and David hold for Jewish readers? What about for Christians?

Jesus as Torah:

5. Reflect on the concept that Jesus equals Torah and Torah equals Jesus, as presented in the chapter. How does this perspective deepen our understanding of Jesus' role in fulfilling the Law and the Prophets?

6. Matthew divided his Gospel into five teaching blocks. What is the significance of this division? How does this connect Jesus to the Torah?

Personal Reflection:

7. Have there been times when you encountered a scripture passage or prophecy that was difficult to understand. How did your perspective change over time, particularly in light of Jesus' life and teachings?

8. Consider the analogy of the "long and winding road" and the simplicity of a child pointing out what was previously unseen.

How does this relate to our journey of understanding Jesus as the Messiah?

9. Discuss ways in which we can share the significance of Jesus as the fulfillment of Old Testament prophecy with others, particularly those who may not be familiar with scripture.

Action Step for Next Week:

In your quiet time, church service, or other study time look for places where you can clearly see Jesus fulfilling the law or prophets. Write them down here:

CHAPTER 2

Mark, What Do You See?

"I See Tragedy in Rudimentary Greek"

LIVING ALONE ON A POLLUTED PLANET

Given the award for most improbable, between the strange man stretched across my lawn gazing into the sky at 2 AM or me scurrying across that same lawn thousands of times without ever stopping to glance up, I'd vote for the latter every time. I certainly would.

What I'm referring to is a legendary family wager. Our trampoline, half-destroyed after 10 years of wear and tear, had to go. All it required, I assured them, was a lean-to poster board in our front yard with one word on it: "Free." "Dad, there's NO WAY anybody wants it. You're going to have to haul it to the dump yourself." The fact they collectively saw me, not we, as the remedy to the problem doubly bugged me. Regardless, the bet was $10 of my dollars to every $1 of theirs that the trampoline would be gone by morning. I would either gloat about collecting their crisp 1-dollar bills or eat $50 worth of crow. I'll admit, it was a close call. Within hours of first light, a subtle clanking roused me from my sleep. The sight of a dad sprawled across my front lawn at 2 AM in the morning, hands crossed behind his head, staring up at the night sky, brought nothing but sheer bliss as I mentally tallied up five crisp $1 bills in my head. The fact that his wife meticulously disassembled the trampoline as he lay there added additional humor.

That is, until a slight degree of shame settled in. Gazing out the front window in the distance, just beyond the stranger's torso, "how weird," I found it, that I had trekked across that same lawn in a perpetually frenzied state and missed what this complete stranger did not: a brief respite to breath pure air and marvel at a pristine sky. That might be what Philip Yancey envisioned when he wrote:

> "Living on a planet of free will and rebellion, Jesus often must have felt 'not at home.' At such times He went aside and prayed, as if to breathe pure air from a life-support system that would give Him the strength to continue living on a polluted planet."

The branch of drama that treats the sorrowful or terrible events encountered by a heroic individual in a dignified style is known as tragedy. As the Greeks developed it, the tragic form, more than any other, raised questions about human existence. Why must humans suffer? Why must humans be forever torn between the seeming irreconcilable forces of good and evil, freedom and necessity, truth and deceit? Are the causes of suffering outside of oneself, in blind chance, in the evil designs of others, in the malice of the gods? Why is justice so elusive? Answers of which may not be found. But some can be for a price: the cost of our precious little time.

Philip Yancey suggested, "Perhaps we should say 'Christ is the pattern' rather than 'Christ is the answer,' because Jesus' own life did not offer the answers most people are looking for." Mark leaned into the tragedy of Jesus' life more than any other. His observations capture how "out of place" Jesus must have felt here. For Aristotle, who lived 384-322 BC, tragedy had a point: to use a character's death to create an emotional effect like pity or fear in the audience, a cleansing or purifying sort of emotional release that he calls catharsis, which Mark's treatment accomplishes. That makes his version of events feel so tragic, like a gut punch without warning, striking at the "veryness of one's soul" (an impactful expression my seminary professor used).

This somber reality caught us by surprise at a men's group in 2022. I felt led to veer away from the lesson notes that night, freelancing on loneliness. In particular, I was discovering how pronounced loneliness is throughout Mark's appraisal, although I'd never noticed it before. Spontaneously, in one of those ultra-rare instances, the entire room felt a collective sense of immense sadness beyond the ordinary. I, for one, did not speak for a long time. Nobody felt comfortable interrupting the silence. Silence, it appears, often knows more of our Lord than speech. I'm not sure I've experienced that more profoundly throughout my life.

"Sorrow," as the thought-provoking devotional *Streams in the Desert* deciphers it, "is God's tool to plow the depths of the soul, that it may yield richer harvests...it is sorrow that causes us to take the time to think deeply and seriously...it takes sorrow to expand and deepen the soul. Sorrow reveals unknown depths of the soul and unknown capacities for suffering and service."

VAIN AND EMPTY PROMISES

In a strict sense, anytime "wilderness" is associated with Jesus (in Mark), we should interpret it as *loneliness*. Loneliness best articulates the barrenness or utter seclusion typical of Christ's life experience. We first see it in Mark's retelling of Christ's temptation in the wilderness.[16] We should expect satan[17] to try and cash in on the perfect storm. "The Spirit impelled Him to go out into the **loneliness**, and He was in the **loneliness** forty days being tempted by satan." (Mark 1:12-13) True to his nature, wasting precious little time as he's prone to do, satan, like a lion on the prowl, pounced on his prey when weakest, cut off

---

[16] In Scripture, a "desert" (érēmos) is ironically also where God richly grants His presence and provision for those seeking Him.

[17] There's nothing proper about satan's name; it will remain uncapitalized throughout.

from the fray. This was a tactic that struck his fancy from days of old; he's oh so crafty, a schemer increasing in cleverness throughout the ages.

Christ had never been more vulnerable than in that instance, and the enemy, as if by nature, got wind of it. With death and decay ominously encroaching, satan circled above like a diseased vulture, methodically swooping down ever nearer his prey. The nearly dead are keenly aware why the vultures are present. Jesus, however hard, did not succumb to the vain and empty promises offered Him. This promise, more or less, was a shortcut to the crown that bypassed the cross.

I'm reminded of the lyrics from a blues musician, Robert Johnson, who sold his soul to the devil at the Crossroads on the outskirts of Clarksville, Mississippi:

From Memphis to Norfolk, is a thirty-six hours ride...(whether Johnson was aware or not, is it estimated Christ endured the cross 36 hours)....... *And when I leave this town, I'm gon' bid you farewell, And when I return again, you'll have a great long story to tell.*

The schemer's fiery darts were by no means retired in the desert. More held at bay until what Luke described as a more "opportune time."[18] The Place of the Skull would present itself sooner rather than later.

PAIN SHARED IS HALVED. PAIN ALONE IS DOUBLED

A respite from the loneliness can scarcely be found. It resumed a short time after Jesus withdrew from the desert in Mark 1:35, "In the early morning, while it was still dark, Jesus got up, left the house,

---

[18] Luke 4:13 - *And so when the devil had finished every temptation, he left Him until an opportune time.*

and went away to a **loneliness** place, and was praying there." And again in 1:45, "Jesus could no longer publicly enter a city, but stayed out in **loneliness** areas; and they (the crowds) were coming to Him from everywhere." It must be noted that it's not like being in a crowd eliminates loneliness. Many of us never feel more alone than when surrounded by others. The multitudes pressing themselves in upon Christ offered no semblance of companionship. It was a sad reality Jesus was well aware of: they would peel off as quickly as they came.

Barely into chapter 2, as disheartening as it sounds, the painful process of abandonment that Jesus undergoes is beginning. Abandonment is like a maze getting smaller and smaller as you go until contact with the outside world is ultimately choked out. The multitudes bailed out first, dwindling down to an audience of zero.

The line was a mile long of people walking away from Christ. At the head of the procession was a mix of Pharisees, Sadducees, Herodians, Scribes, Zealots, and Sanhedrin. They were followed closely by the people who had been physically touched by God and healed...so much for once being His biggest fans! His immediate family isn't immune to our scrutiny either. Surely, they toughed it out and stood by His side? Not at all. Chapter 3 records their shockingly premature exit.[19] "And when his family heard it, they went out to seize him, for they were saying, 'He is out of his mind.'" (Mark 3:21 ESV). Don't you love the fact Scripture doesn't sanitize its heroes?

The circle of 12 lingered a bit longer, like fair-weather friends biding their time to see how things panned out before casting their lots one way or another. I'm not sure how much was lost here. The Disciples were either incapable of understanding Jesus up to this point or refused to try. I can't imagine the sorrow of living your entire life not feeling understood.

---

[19] *And when his family heard it, they went out to seize him, for they were saying, "He is out of his mind." ESV* – Mark 3:21

Western novelist Stephen Bly says that in America's Old West, there were two types of friends: runners and standers.

> At the first sign of trouble, the runner would bolt—abandoning you to whatever peril you were facing. But a stander would stick with you no matter the circumstances. Unfortunately, you wouldn't know which kind of friend you had until trouble came. And then it was too late—unless your friend was a stander. (Be a Stander, OurDailyBread.com)

The runners included Judas, who succumbed to temptation first. Quickly following on his heels came eight more disciples. The three that remained, Peter, James, and John, were holdouts, at least temporarily. But in the Garden of Gethsemane, none obeyed our Lord in His most desperate time of need:

> "My soul is deeply grieved to the point of death; remain here and keep watch…" And He came the third time, and said to them, "Are you still sleeping and resting? It is enough; the hour has come; behold, the Son of Man is being betrayed into the hands of sinners" (Mark 14:34; 41).

In the end, Peter, who swore up and down to be a stander, proved to be a runner. He denied any association with Christ and refused to even utter His Name. "I do not know this man you are talking about!" (Mark 14:71)

Another note before moving on that's always bothered me—Jesus was bare on the cross for all the world to see. He had no loincloth, no way to cover Himself with His hands. His arms had already been nailed down. That's just so sad. Utterly humiliating. Could it have possibly gotten worse? The answer is pitiful; yes, much worse.

AN AUDIENCE OF NONE

I've heard people say that true worship is directed towards an audience of One. Although the crucifixion was the ultimate act of worship, we can rightly say it was an audience of none. For six intolerable hours, God turned away from the nastiness and filth heaped upon Jesus' shoulders. It was only fitting for Him to do so because God is holy, defined more by what it isn't than what it is- that which is separate from the ordinary or mundane. To say God is holy, holy, holy, heralds just how wide the chasm had grown between them. With no life support system breathing pure air into His lungs, He couldn't possibly survive living on our polluted planet.

OFFICIAL TIME OF DEATH: 3:00 PM FRIDAY, 30 A.D.

Thousands upon thousands of Middle Easterners had the privilege of seeing, hearing, even feeling the skin of God—as hard as that is to fathom-all without filter...the renowned Galilean named Jesus.

As I read Mark's record, I try to overhear, behind the written text, the steady volley of bold assertions by His would-be adherents—vowing to carry crosses at The Nazarene's first bidding, follow Him at all costs, even die as His martyrs in hopes of changing the world as they knew it. At 3:00 PM that Good Friday, 30 AD, that storyline ended. How sorrowed The King of Kings must have felt as He scanned Golgotha, ominously nicknamed "The Place of the Skull," saddened at how devoid it was of all those would-be followers. All but a few handfuls among those tens of thousands remained: "At the first sign of trouble, the runner would bolt— abandoning you to whatever peril you were facing."

THE STRANGE NOTION OF PITYING GOD

> By any measure, Jesus led a tragic life: rumors of illegitimacy, taunts of insanity from His family, rejection by most who heard Him, betrayal by His friends, the savage turn of a mob against Him, a series of justice-mocking trials, execution in a form reserved for slaves and violent criminals. A pitiful story, to be sure, and that is the heart of the scandal: we do not expect to pity God. (Philip Yancey)

To anyone seeking union with Jesus from Mark's vantage point, it is nothing short of seeking anguish. It's hard to single out a more tragic historical figure to unite oneself with. 700 years before Christ's birth, an ancient prophet tried to prepare us for what lay ahead. The markings of Messiahship were to look like this: "He was...A Man of Sorrows, acquainted with the deepest grief. We turned our backs on Him and looked the other way. He was despised, and we did not care" (Is. 53:3 NLT). When slapped, spat upon, and ridiculed, the Messiah would refuse to defend Himself, much less retaliate (Is. 50:6), what He phrased as "turning the other cheek."

We didn't want it to be that way, then or now. Strength, like that of a warrior wielding his mighty sword, is the preferred prerequisite for any brave soul who might lead us into the fray. The exact antithesis would be gentle, lowly, meek, and mild, all of which feel counterintuitive for adjectives worthy of the Leader among us. Even Mark 10:45, widely regarded as the verse that best typifies his summation, appears anticlimactic: "For even the Son of Man did not come to be served, but to serve, and to give His life as a ransom for many." And yet, in a strangely poetic way, God's preferred method of establishing strength has always been through apparent weakness, either His or ours. Consider how:

- "From the mouth of infants and nursing babes You have established strength because of Your adversaries, To make the enemy and the revengeful cease" (Psalm 8:2).

- Imagine wolves, lions, and leopards yielding to the hand of a child in the Messianic Reign, while the nursing infant is amused playing over the cobra's den. Isaiah 11:6; 8, "And the wolf will dwell with the lamb, And the leopard will lie down with the kid, And the calf and the young lion and the fatling together; And *a little boy* will lead them...*The nursing child* will play by the hole of the cobra, And *the weaned child* will put his hand on the viper's den."

In essence, the weakness of God supersedes the strength of man. (1 Cor. 1:25). But we cannot let that negate the tragedy Mark saw and unfolded for us in rudimentary Greek. The very Person to be pitied at the heart of the scandal is none other than God's own Son.

Discussion Questions for "Mark, What Do You See?"

Look Back:

Share the instances you saw Jesus in the OT during the past week.

Tragedy, Human Existence, and Isolation:

1. This chapter highlights the theme of misunderstanding and rejection of Jesus by those closest to Him. How does this theme resonate with your own experiences of faith and relationships?

2. Have you ever experienced doubt or skepticism from your own family or religious community regarding your beliefs or decisions? How did you handle it?

3. Loneliness is a recurring theme in the Gospel of Mark. What can we learn about facing loneliness from Jesus' example?

The Temptation in the Wilderness:

4. Reflect on Jesus' temptation in the wilderness as described in Mark 1:12-13. How does this event demonstrate Jesus' vulnerability and the tactics of the adversary?

5. How does Jesus' resistance to temptation provide guidance for us in facing our own trials? See Hebrews 2:17-18 and 4:15 for insight into this question.

The Concept of Pitying God:

6. The text discusses the notion of pitying God, especially in the context of Jesus' suffering and crucifixion. Why is it challenging for people to reconcile the idea of God experiencing sorrow and suffering?

7. The chapter explores the paradox of strength in weakness, highlighting how God's power is often manifested through apparent weakness. How does Jesus' willingness to endure suffering and humiliation demonstrate this principle? How does this perspective challenge our conventional understanding of strength?

Action Steps for Next Week:

Is there someone that may have felt abandoned by you? Are you willing to reach out to them in the next seven days and ask for forgiveness? If yes, get the group to pray for follow through.

Have you felt abandoned by someone or ever felt lonely in the presence of others? Are you able to forgive them in person? If not, write a letter here to help you process your feelings and hurt.

Dear_____,

_____

_____

_____

_____

_____

_____

_____

_____

_____

Sincerely,

Think of three standers who stood by your side when the whole world seemed to have walked out. Unpack the story with your study group. Commit to calling, texting, or emailing each stander to say how meaningful it was when they stuck by your side. Hold each other accountable by reporting back their responses the next time you meet.

CHAPTER 3

Luke, What Do You See?

"I See Those Otherwise Unseen"

GETTING PICKED LAST OR NOT GETTING PICKED AT ALL

At least initially, Cindy thought she got picked last, or not picked at all, due to her being a girl. That was until girls were selected to be team captains when teams were divided up in grade school. Four square, kickball, and capture the flag were always the same. It was one thing to get looked over by gross boys or stuck-up girls, but being "unseen" by your two closest friends when they got selected captains...? That stung worst of all. Someone once said, *"That feeling you get in your stomach when your heart is broken, it's like all the butterflies just died."* For Cindy, the butterflies kept dying over and over again, every recess, every day. It got so old.

No matter how hard she coached herself up, "I can do this! Quit messing up!", it made no difference. Either the hand-eye coordination was off, or the athleticism was lacking. Things got so pitiful she could quote only one mantra to herself: "Oh please, please, please, whatever you do, don't pick me last," as if the team captains could read her mind. And there was a reason her fear of getting picked last was no longer an issue. You see, starting in 2nd grade, Cindy stopped getting picked at all.

Did you know? "Feeling rejected is not much different from actual pain. MRI scans have shown that the same areas of the brain that respond to *physical pain also react to being hurt by rejection. As far as your brain is concerned, a broken heart is no different than a broken arm.*" – didyouknowblog.com

The Gospel of Luke best captures God's affinity for down-and-outers, like Cindy, more than any book of the Bible—the dregs, the marginalized, the looked over, the looked down upon, and the most heartbreaking of all—the people who felt unseen by society. And yet, it was this crowd who comprised Jesus' favorite segment of society to linger among. It was the first time in history that the misfits got picked first, not last, of all.

THE CALL PLACED UPON HIM

This brings to mind a story about a small-town preacher from long ago who always knew, as far back as he could recall, that God had placed "the call" on his life to administer hope to the world. While other boys his age envisioned what they wanted to be when they grew up and how they might earn a respectable living, he aspired towards higher ideals, forfeiting whatever was necessary to make an everlasting impact—in fact, to alter history.

Many often wonder, "How do you know if you're called to full-time ministry?" Well, in this case, this Preacher knew alright. It's good to reiterate by saying, he just knew; I can assure you of that. But in any case, it was the oppressed—today we deem them "underdogs"—who found themselves on the receiving end of his affections; they pretty much comprised his target audience. Understandably so if you think about it, because his message of hope takes on extra significance for the ones who've never experienced it before.

If you inquired among ministers, "How intimidating is it to preach in strange lands among complete strangers," the majority would concur, "It's not that bad." But if asked as a follow-up, "What about returning to your hometown and preaching among those who know you best?" "Well," they'd assure you, "that's an entirely different matter." Aside from His doting mother, who assured all that her son could do no wrong, most everyone in town predicted that the man of God in question would amount to little, especially with no proper schooling or high standing to speak of. How true is the statement that stems from long ago, "Not even a prophet is welcome in his hometown"?

The assembled congregants sat captive, eager to hear, maybe even critique his opening remarks. Rumor had it that he'd worked on this particular message for the better part of 30 years. For some, this was "overkill" for time spent preparing sermons; it was a moot issue for others more concerned to see if his theology was proper or not. But for the tiny minority comprising his target audience, they were poised to hear the most genuinely compelling words of a lifetime.

That morning, the attendant in the sanctuary meticulously unrolled the sacred parchments, placing the ancient Torah in the Preacher's palm and turning to a selected reading from Isaiah. How pleasant that sacred scroll must have felt in His hand. The divine irony got lost on almost all. It's funny now, in hindsight, knowing that each letter, stroke, jot, and tittle of that Torah in Jesus' hometown synagogue was handwritten by Him from long ago. The first prophetic statement from the world's Savior, Jesus Christ, resounded like this[20]: "The Spirit of the Lord is upon Me, because He anointed Me to preach the Gospel

---

[20] This was the first prophetic statement of Jesus' public ministry that began when He was 30 years of age.

to the poor. He has sent Me to proclaim release to the captives, and recovery of sight to the blind, to set free those who are oppressed, to proclaim the favorable year of the Lord." (Luke 4:18-19)

Did you make the connection? Finally! This was the precise moment that the misfits got picked first, not last, of all.

MISFITS AND UNDERDOGS

Chapter four of Luke's ordering of events isn't the first time Christ's predisposition toward outsiders is seen. He clues us in with earlier hints, none of which were subtle to 1st-century readers, that pop up at the outset in chapters one and two. In eyebrow-raising fashion, women predominate the birth-narrative. Mary, mentioned explicitly by name thirteen times, and Elizabeth nine times, are on full display as heroines of the show.[21] Whether we as modern readers like it or not, women's roles took a major back seat when Scripture was written. Lists commonly included males only, not females (feeding the 5,000 as a headcount only took into consideration the number of men present). As for tracing your family tree or figuring out your ancestry, you could forget trying to find out who the women were. All genealogies of the day, including the ones recorded in the Bible and outside of it, were exclusively men. That is until we turn the page to Luke chapter three.

For the only time in Scripture, ladies' names pop up in a birth record. This is not just any birth account, but that of the long-awaited Jewish King in Luke 3. And it gets far more risqué. Luke traced Jesus' lineage through His mother, Mary; unlike Matthew, who traced Jesus through His stepfather Joseph. Luke inserts the names of three more women for a total of four, two of whom were women of ill-repute! A tell-all of that sort was nothing short of abhorrent in the minds of most.

---

[21]   Mary's name appears eight times in chapter one, and five times in chapter two. Elizabeth appears nine times in chapter one.

As to the financial backers of Jesus' itinerate preaching ministry? Make no mistake; that'd be women who underwrote it.[22] What about the handful of brave souls tough enough to watch the brutality of Christ's cross in full? That award also goes to women.[23] Luke's star witnesses of the resurrection? Women, in particular Mary Magdalene, purportedly a prostitute in her previous life.[24]

Luke was on a roll, so why stop there? Considering that he was the only Gentile writer in Scripture and the only New Testament author not to see Jesus, Luke must have felt like an outsider looking in. It's no wonder he keyed in on fellow outsiders like shepherds outside the city limits far out in the fields. While you and I may hold mental depictions of shepherds revered and admired by their contemporaries, nothing could be further from the truth. At the time of Christ's birth, shepherds could not give credible testimony in court, irrespective of how heinous of an act they'd witnessed. Shepherds were banned from freely entering houses of worship. They had to avoid physical contact with all others. In essence, they were legally, spiritually, and physically cut off from the general public at large.

> Luke 5:31 - "It is not those who are healthy who need a physician, but those who are sick."

How compelling must it have been for those very shepherds to be told by an Angel of the Lord, "Today, in the city of David there has been born **for you** a Savior, who is Christ the Lord."[25] Not "born for you

---

[22]   Luke 8:1-3
[23]   John the Apostle is the only male figure we're made aware of present during Christ's crucifixion.
[24]   Luke 24:1-2
[25]   Luke 2:11

all" as in a collective sense, but individually.[26] You can almost imagine hearing a shepherd muttering to himself, "Wait a minute, did I hear correctly...the long-awaited Savior was born specifically for me?" According to the messengers of God, the answer was a resounding, "Yes! He came just for you." That, in my estimation, is the Bible's most touching and poignant account.

GOD IS TILTED TOWARD THE UNDERDOG

As for the Angel of the Lord's birth announcement, there was more. It seems the Lord was intent on lavishing the shepherds with grace upon grace. Following this notice, the angel was joined by a heavenly host ensemble; none but shepherds comprised the audience. And last, but by no means least, who first got to peer into the cave or stable to behold God's Son? You guessed it. The shepherds! I completely agree with Philip Yancey's assessment: "As I read the birth stories about Jesus, I cannot help but conclude that though the world may be tilted toward the rich and powerful, God is tilted toward the underdog."

Amy Dickinson observed, *"There is nothing more painful than being rejected simply for being who you are."* That is true, but I would add, *"There is nothing more beautiful than being accepted simply for being who you are."* In a world that is all too busy and often overlooks the unseen, Jesus' affection for the misfits, the marginalized, and the broken reflects a profound love that sees beauty where others may see flaws. There's hope for everyone, especially for those who feel unseen.

Hardly a page gets flipped in Luke without identifying references to down-and-outers. To make the point, while at the same time testing your Bible knowledge, see which of the following you can answer:[27]

---

[26] "You" is in the second-person singular.

[27] ANSWERS: a) Magi b) Zacchaeus c) a Gentile named Simon of Cyrene d) a criminal on the cross, who moments earlier had hurled abuse/insults - at Christ e) a Roman

Keep in mind the shock-worthy nature of each claim Luke was intent on including.

a)   The first Christ-worshippers?

b)   Jesus commended this chief tax-collector as "a son of Abraham"[28]

c)   Who was the only human in history to physically carry the cross of Christ?

d)   Who was one of the first, if not the very first person to hear, "Well done thy good and faithful servant"?

e)   Throughout all Israel, who was the man with the greatest faith of all?[29]

f)   Of the 10 lepers Jesus cleansed, only one (a foreigner) returned to thank him. What region was he from?

g)   In one of Jesus' parables, what type of Samaritan was heralded as a hero? You may recall, he was the one who stopped and noticed, unlike all the other passerby. I'll go ahead and give you the answer to this one. It was the Good Samaritan, not the pious priest or Levite who walked right by.

Isn't it fitting that in Luke 14, the same cast of characters (like those listed above) are gathered around an exquisite banquet table hosted by Christ Himself? Society's "ins" were the first to receive dinner invitations; each, however, allowing the cares and concerns of this world to take precedence over the Host, politely declined:

· *The first one said, 'I have bought a piece of land and I need to go out and look at it; please consider me excused.'*

Centurion (non-Jew) f) Samaria

[28] Luke 19:9

[29] Luke 7:6-9

- Another one said, 'I have bought five yoke of oxen, and I am going to try them out; please consider me excused.'

- Another one said, 'I have married a wife, and for that reason I cannot come.'

Undeterred, the Head of the household demanded: "'Go out at once into the streets and lanes of the city and bring in here the poor and crippled and blind and lame.' And the slave said, 'Master, what you commanded has been done, and still there is room.' And the master said to the slave, 'Go out into the highways and along the hedges, and compel them to come in, *so that my house may be filled.*'" (Luke 14:21-23). If I were to give my best guess for, "Luke, what did you see?" I'd go with that banquet table. Christ seated at the head, dining among and delighting in the otherwise unseen. Luke included it for a reason. Yeah, that's it. That's what he saw.

AN ABSOLUTE MASTERPIECE

Every year, thousands of tourists visit Chartres Cathedral in France, long renowned as one of Europe's most beautiful and historically significant cathedrals. Underneath its shadow, high upon a hill that overlooks the monumental Cathedral, sits a lone little house, unnoteworthy for the most part and mainly out of sight. Most travelers miss the folk-art site La Maison Picassiette, The House of Millions of Pieces. Its history dates back to 1938, when its owner, Raymond Isadore, began collecting broken pieces of glass, pottery, and bottle caps in a nearby field that others had thrown away. He started decorating the exterior of his little house with brilliant mosaics of colorful broken pieces. He then covered the interior (even furniture) with shimmering pieces as well. Finally, he designed a chapel depicting images of Jesus and a replica of Chartres Cathedral and its surrounding town — his vantage-point from his beloved hilltop house. He continued adding to his mosaic home until he died in 1964.

What was once disregarded as garbage, Monsieur Isadore repurposed into astonishing works of art. Whereas others saw trash, Isadore beheld innate beauty underneath, absolute masterpieces that needed to be brought out. That sounds a lot like Jesus.

Has someone crushed your spirit beyond repair? Is your life fragmented to pieces? Is your ego obliterated? Is your heart wrecked in half? Are you void of all pride in life presently? I assure you, He sees you. You are not going unnoticed. "Wait a minute, did I hear correctly?" You may be thinking, much like the shepherds. The answer is a resounding, "Yes!" Like Raymond Isadore's Picassiette House, the most incredible beauty is often found in the looked-over, passed-by — and yes — broken people and places. During His time on earth, Jesus picked up the shattered pieces of those beaten down beyond recognition and made them one-of-a-kind mosaics. They didn't come out as before, but even better. They looked more like Him.

Discussion Questions for "Luke, What Do You See?"

Look Back:

If you did reach out to someone who may have felt abandoned by you how did they respond?

Report back how each of your three standers reacted after hearing from you.

Reflection on Rejection:

1. Take a moment to reflect on your own life. Have there been times when you have felt unseen or rejected? How might

God be inviting you to see yourself and others differently in light of his love and acceptance?

2. Explore the theme of being overlooked in the Bible. Can you think of other biblical characters or passages that reflect similar experiences to Cindy's?

3. Discuss instances in the Gospels where Jesus interacted with or showed favor towards the marginalized and the outcasts of society. What do these stories reveal about God's character?

4. Comment on the following: Amy Dickinson observed, "*There is nothing more painful than being rejected simply for being who you are.*" That is true, but I would add, "*There is nothing more beautiful than being accepted simply for being who you are.*"

The Role of Women and the Significance of Shepherds:

5. Consider the significant roles played by women in Luke's narrative, from Mary and Elizabeth to the female financial backers of Jesus' ministry. How does Luke challenge societal norms of his time through his portrayal of women?

6. Explore the cultural and religious significance of shepherds in biblical times. How does Jesus' choice to reveal his birth to shepherds challenge societal expectations and demonstrate God's love for the marginalized?

Finding Beauty in Brokenness:

7. Analyze the parable of the banquet in Luke 14. What does this parable teach us about God's desire to reach out to those

who are often overlooked or marginalized? What changes should that parable bring about in us?

8.   How does the story of Raymond Isadore's Picassiette House illustrate God's ability to transform brokenness into beauty, and what hope does it offer to those who are hurting?

Action Steps for Next Week:

Be on the lookout this week for three individuals who might feel unseen or overlooked. Pick out a skill or talent you admire about them. Send a quick "Just so you know" note to commend them for it. As an example: "Sydney! Just so you know, I've always appreciated how well you _____. Hope you smile knowing it never goes unnoticed!" Consider adding a Bible verse like Proverbs 17:17, 1 Thess. 5:11, or 1 Cor. 15:58. Report back to the group the situation and the response the next time you meet.

Take it one step further: Find an opportunity to show you care for someone. Buy someone a coffee and take time talking with them. Invite a coworker to lunch if you see them eating alone at their desk. Find out someone's interests and talk with them about them.

CHAPTER 4

John, What Do You See?

"I See God"

An enormous chunk of roughly hewn marble known as "The Giant" was abandoned in the Opera del Duomo courtyard for 25 years. The two artists originally commissioned to sculpt an Old Testament figure to guard the Florence Cathedral in Italy snubbed their noses at the unsightly monstrosity claiming, "What good can come from the quarries of Carrara" due to the marble's blatant imperfections. Then, in 1501, a new day dawned when an up-and-coming sculptor entered the arena. Had other artisans been asked, "What do you see?" while standing beneath the 13,000-pound, 14-foot eyesore, their collective gasps would have been entirely negative. Not so with the 26-year-old hired to complete the project, fresh off his failed attempt at art fraud. He would later famously say about his sculptures: "Every block of stone contains a statue inside, and it is the task of the sculptor to release it" and also, "I saw the angel in the marble and carved until I set it free." With his completed work unveiled four years later, on September 8th, 1504, the rest of the world could finally behold what the world's greatest sculptor, Michelangelo, envisioned all along: "I created a vision of David in my mind and simply carved away everything that was not David...I give you *David*."

In the 1st Century, many people looked at Jesus with less regard than a clump of stone. Among His countrymen, He was on the receiving end of countless barrages including: He's a mere carpenter and nothing more, He is lacking in education,[30] "Can any good thing come from Nazareth?"[31] Some gave subtle hints of an illegitimate birth, "Is this not Mary's son,"[32] the crowds quipped. Children were customarily tied to fathers, never mothers. Others flat-out claimed, "He has a demon and is insane!" [33] Even Jesus' closest relatives once remarked, "He is out of His mind!"[34]

However, a follower named John, self-described as the one whom Jesus loved, saw something different. Whereas Matthew saw the Jewish Messiah, Mark the Son of God, and Luke the Son of Man, when beholding Christ, John saw what few others (if any) saw. He saw God. Akin to Michelangelo's, "I give you David," John tells us, "I give you God."

EXIT STAGE LEFT

In the 1990's, I spent six weeks in New Jersey training for a pharmaceutical job. One Broadway play I attended in New York was *The Phantom of the Opera*. Witnessing such a tremendous consortium of props and characters filling one grand stage was enthralling. One by one, at various stages, lesser roles would roll off, or "exit stage left," which is a directive used in theater to guide actors on and off stage. It is defined as, "a timely exit done so as not to make a scene or attract attention to oneself." [35]

It took some initial guesswork to predict which character might eventually be propelled to center stage. But with every musical or production, there does come a definitive moment, at a precise juncture, when audience members can first determine who the show's Star is: "Oh, there he is, that's him, he's the main one." In

[30] Mark 6:2-3
[31] John 1:46
[32] Mark 6:3
[33] John 10:20
[34] Mark 3:21
[35] thefreedictionary.com

Phantom, that took a good while to figure out. Not so with John's synopsis. Before the opening curtain parts, and long before the first flick of a spotlight switch, John catapults the Star of his narrative to his audience in line one of chapter one: "In the beginning was the Word, and the Word was with God, and the Word was God" (John 1:1).

With this as our starting point, we can liken John's treatment of Jesus to divine drama. From the curtain first rising in the opening act (i.e., John 1:1) to its conclusion in John 21:25, "There are also many other things which Jesus did, which if they were written in detail, I suppose that even the world itself would not contain the books that would be written," John's attention is exclusively fixated on Christ. The center stage, which is always front and center in this account, is unabashedly reserved for Christ, whose glory is not to be shared with another. I can assure you that every other character in John's narration views Him in precisely that light. We could relegate 100% of what follows (including people, places, and things) to supporting cast members. Much like poetry from Shakespeare:

> All the world's a stage,
> And all the men and women merely players;
> They have their exits and their entrances;

Or lyrics from my favorite rock band Rush:

> All the world's indeed a stage
> And we are merely players
> Performers and portrayers

Who else gets cast by John in that light?

- Let's start with John the Baptizer—the best supporting actor, a role he wholeheartedly embraced. The Baptist was honored by the most fantastic accolade in history[36] and yet

---

[36] "Truly I say to you, among those born of women there has not arisen anyone greater than John the Baptist! Yet the one who is least in the kingdom of heaven is greater than he." Matthew 11:11

how happy he was to see his role diminish so long as Jesus' role didn't. "He must increase, but I must decrease" (John 3:30), and, "He who is coming after me has proved to be my superior because He existed before me" (John 1:30).

- Mary, Jesus' mother, is the best supporting actress. When consulted about the social faux pas of running out of wine in John 2, she was emphatic, "Whatever Jesus says to do, do that!" A consideration both Catholics and Protestants can agree upon.

- The miracles, which we'll look at more closely, get the briefest of nods, appearing more like credits relegated to the end of movie reels. The point is to Whom they point; never were they intended to be an end unto themselves. "The very works that I do— testify[37] about Me, that the Father has sent Me" (John 5:36).

- Or what about God the Holy Spirit, equal to the Father and Jesus in all respects? He delights to deflect the spotlight off Himself and beam it upon the Son. The Helper, or Holy Spirit, Jesus promised, "will teach you all things, and bring to your remembrance all that I said to you" (John 14:26). And again in John 15:26, "When the Helper comes, whom I will send to you from the Father, that is the Spirit of truth who proceeds from the Father, He will testify about Me." Notice how the Spirit brings to remembrance the words of Jesus, not of His own, and "testifies" of Jesus, not of Himself. Both verses are characteristic of the reflecting and redirecting I've already discussed.

---

[37] Testify is defined universally as that by which a person or a thing is distinguished from others and known.

John tirelessly eases all else, including inanimate objects such as the Temple and miraculous acts such as healings, off to the theater's side. He allows nothing and no one to distort his view of Jesus.

JUDAISM'S CENTERPIECE

Picture the enormity of Herod's Temple for a moment and how it must have cast its large shadow across Jerusalem. Then consider how dwarfed the colossal structure appeared when juxtaposed against our Lord? In John's eyes, potential adherents to Jesus' message must fix their gaze on His person rather than bricks and mortar. You may recall the time Jesus upended the moneychanger's tables, chasing away the merchants *and* their livestock with a whip. He became enraged at the mockery made of His Father's house. The bystanders insisted in John 2:18-20, "What sign do You show us as your authority for doing these things?" "Destroy this temple, and in three days I will raise it up" Jesus replied. "The Jews then said, 'It took forty-six years to build this temple, and will You raise it up in three days?' But He was speaking of **the Temple of His body."** Again, the Temple, the centerpiece of the Jewish religion, had to exit stage left, "so as not to make a scene or attract attention to oneself," since the Messiah had arrived. At that point, the Temple's ultimate purpose, pointing to the coming Messiah, was complete. Then, finally, in 70 AD, the bricks and mortar ceased to exist when Titus, the Roman Emperor, besieged Jerusalem and obliterated its Temple.

John incessantly fixates on the Lord in many ways. In one such instance, he recalls a story in the history of Persian kings. When the wife of one of the generals of Cyrus—the king mentioned in Isaiah— was charged with treason and condemned to die, the husband went before Cyrus, fell on his face and said, "*Oh Lord, take my life instead of hers. Let me die in her place.*" Cyrus said, "*Love like that must not be spoiled by death.*" As the couple walked away, the husband asked his wife, "*Did you notice how kindly the king looked upon us when he gave you the pardon?*" The wife replied, "*I had no eyes for the king. I saw only the man willing to die in my place."* That story was like a precursor to words penned by the Apostle some 600 years later: *"Greater love has no one than this, that one lay down His life for His friends."* [38]

ATTESTING SIGNS

What about the miraculous? What treatment did John give there? Let's face it. Granting sight to someone born blind or restoring a person who's been dead four days back to life were showstopper, for sure. The multitudes persisted in shoving them to the fore. John did not. It feels like he perfectly executes an honest man's version of bait and switch with no ill intent. The crowd gets captivated by the extraordinary and, within seconds, John walks the script down and lays it at the feet of Jesus. Where do we see that? It's within the text.

Rather than using the term *miracle* for Jesus' supernatural acts, John diverges from Matthew, Mark, and Luke by employing a different expression: *attesting* signs (*martur* in Greek), which means "to testify that a thing is so, to commend or give a good report." It's interesting to note that the Greek *martur* is the same word the Risen Christ gave when commissioning His disciples to spread His message: "But you will receive power when the Holy Spirit has come upon you; and you shall be my **witnesses** (*martur*) in Jerusalem, Judea, Samaria and even the remotest part of the earth!"[39] Witnesses literally read, "You will be my martyrs." Over time, witnesses got killed for spreading their faith, thereby being deemed "martyrs." But if we return to attesting signs, they're defined as authenticating or confirming something beyond themselves.[40] When an airline sends a confirmation that your seat is reserved on such and such flight, they're not sending the cushioned

---

[38] John 15:13
[39] Acts 1:8
[40] sēmeíon – a sign (typically miraculous), given especially to confirm, corroborate or authenticate. sēmeíon ("sign") then emphasizes the end-purpose which exalts the one giving it. / of miracles and wonders by which God authenticates the men sent by Him

seat itself, but confirming the seat is there and you get to sit in it. In the same way, acts like Jesus' miracles confirm Him, <u>nothing else</u>. If we continue with the analogy, we might envision a banquet table instead of airplane seats, with reserved seating of its own. Invitations get sent, and whoever is willing can dine with Him. (Rev. 3:20)

NUMBER 7

Next, to emphasize Who the signs pointed to without detracting from their miraculous nature, John had a decision to make. How many of those confirming acts should he pull out of the storehouses of material at his disposal? We'll look at that next; but in advance, if we are the pupils and he's the instructor, we cannot ignore the clapping hands saying, "Listen up! Listen up!"

If we back up for a minute and breakdown the context of the Torah, (the Torah being the basis on which Judaism's belief systems were built), we discover *numbers* meant something; they were totally packed, layered with meaning-much more so than in our day. It is much like a school teacher clapping her hands, saying, "Listen up, listen up," or blinking lights on a car's dashboard: "You must pay attention to this!" From my point of view, the number seven stands out head and shoulders above most numbers recorded in Scripture. Seven signifies fullness, entirely whole or complete. John witnessed many miracles, but true to form, he only chose seven to tell us about. I believe John was driving home the point Jesus is "fully, wholly, completely" who He claims to be-God. The miracles times 7 solidify that point!

If you're tempted to think, "Well, that's just a coincidence," or that too much is being read into this, there's an additional number 7 we must acknowledge, which ties all of John's dissertation together. You'll have to wait until part 2 to unpack this in detail, but for the time being, please know John highlights Jesus claims to be God seven times in seven different ways. This is a clear example of how God is in the details, much more so than "the devil's in them," as so many people exclaim.

In answer to the question, "John, what do you see?", I love C. S. Lewis's observation that will close us out: "As long as you notice and have to count the steps, you are not yet dancing but only learning to dance. A good shoe is a shoe you don't have to notice. Good reading becomes possible when you need not consciously think about eyes, or light, or print, or spelling. The perfect church service would be one we were almost unaware of; our attention would have been on God."[41] From this, I would conclude, the perfect chronicling of Jesus of Nazareth's life would be one we were almost unaware of; our attention would have been exclusively on God. John's Gospel achieves just that.

Discussion Questions for "John, What Do You See?"

Look Back:

Update the group on the responses you received after sending your three "Just so you know" notes. Was it awkward or welcomed? What did you say? If you met with someone in person, share with the group.

Reflection on Michelangelo and "The Giant" Marble:

1. How does the story of Michelangelo and "The Giant" marble reflect the concept of seeing potential where others see imperfection?

2. In what ways can this story be applied to our perception of ourselves and others in light of God's transformative power?

---

[41] *Letters to Malcolm, Chiefly on Prayer.* Lewis, C. S.

Comparing Jesus to the Marble:

3. What lessons can we draw from Michelangelo's approach to sculpting and apply them to how we view and approach Jesus in our lives?

John's Narrative Focus:

4. Why do you think John consistently redirects attention away from secondary characters and events towards Jesus?

5. How can we apply John's approach to our own lives, ensuring that Jesus remains the central focus amidst distractions and competing priorities?

John's Use of "Attesting Signs":

6. How does viewing Jesus' miracles as "attesting signs" impact our understanding of their purpose and significance?

Jesus' Claims to Divinity in John's Gospel:

7. How does understanding Jesus' divinity as presented in John's Gospel influence our belief and relationship with Him?

8. Reflect on C.S. Lewis's observation about noticing and counting steps in dancing. How can we apply this concept to our understanding and experience of God in our lives?

9. Discuss practical ways we can ensure that Jesus remains the central focus in our personal lives, relationships, and ministries, similar to John's approach in his Gospel.

Action Step for Next Week:

This will take some time, but draw up on paper how your life might appear to an audience if played out on center stage. Categorize what the cast of characters would look like in order of prominence. Who or what stands out most? Include those individuals behind the scenes that others might not see but help you live out your life.

BACKSTAGE

CHARACTER

PART II

What Do You Want Us To See?

CHAPTER 5

What Do You Want Us to See, Matthew?

"See Immanuel"

On October 4th, 1995, Hurricane Opal was bearing down off Alabama's coast, ravaging toward my home in Montgomery. Typical for those preparing for storms, I decided on a last-minute dash to the local grocery store. Running to get in and out as quickly as possible, I couldn't help but notice a tiny kitty-cat hiding underneath the car beside me. The kitten must have been the runt of the litter due to its small size. With an impending storm approaching, there was precious little time to coax this kitty into safety.

Predictably, each time I bent down on the car's left side, the kitty rapidly scurried to the right. Whenever I knelt in the back, it dashed towards the front. I was growing exasperated after no less than ten vain attempts to help. My last option was to purchase cat food, the kind with real meat. Unfortunately, not even cat food worked since it was coming from the hand of a larger and stranger species like me. As I drove away, Opal's outer bands of wind and rain had forcefully arrived.

Here I am all these years later, and as crazy as it sounds, I can vividly recall the helpless feeling of trying to help a soaked and shivering little creature only to scare it away. What was needed was another kitten, or even a cat, to have led the kitten out of the storm. Anyone else, or anything else, would only have further frightened it away.

If you only get one take-away from this story, please know this: the most repeated command in Scripture is "Do not fear!" Despite the severity of the storm you are facing, you most assuredly have a Rescuer. His Name is Jesus of Nazareth, who can lead you to safety. However, and this is a very significant however, you can't run away from His voice when He calls. Remember, you can trust Him. Oh, most assuredly, you can. "Take courage! It is I! Do not be afraid!" (Mt. 14:27)

> There is a God who runs to the weary, the worn, and the weak. And the same gentle hands that hold me when I'm broken, they conquer death to bring me victory. (Mullen, Nicole. "My Redeemer Lives")

In many instances where God appeared to His people, they reacted the same way as that kitten. When the "thunder roared, and lightning flashed on Mount Sinai," it utterly horrified the Israelites (Ex. 19:16) to envision themselves falling into the hands of an angry God. "So terrible was the sight that Moses blurted out, 'I am full of fear and trembling.'"[42] The Chosen People kept retreating farther and farther, feeling pinned down and starting to panic, pleading for Moses to speak to them, but not God, "otherwise we will die!"[43]

There was also the time Isaiah beheld the Lord "sitting on a throne, lofty and exalted....and the thresholds trembled at the voice of him who called out!" at which point he entirely fell to pieces exclaiming: "Woe is me, for I am undone!" (Is. 6) But then, everything changed. Scientist J. Robert Oppenheimer once said, "The best way to send an idea is to wrap it up in a person!" But oh, was Christ's arrival so much more than an idea! It was, in Matthew's introductory word, Elohim with us, or Immanuel.

---

[42] Hebrews 12:21;
[43] Exodus 20:18-19

Matthew gives the reader an early impression that Jesus is God with flesh on (Matthew 1:22-23). The invisible God of the skies could be felt physically and interacted with face-to-face. Peals of thunder cracking, smoke rising from the inner cores of mountains, lightning bolts flashing, and deafening trumpets blaring were a far cry from the soft and gentle arrival of an infant Prince on the outskirts of town. How foreign the thought of cradling Mount Sinai's God. It's easy to take for granted the Christmas story getting told to us once a year; for friends of Matthew, it was heard for the first time in history.[44]

Effectively, our precious Redeemer lavished unbridled adoration upon humankind by becoming human. Because people could see and touch God for the very first time, "being born in the likeness of men, and found in appearance as a man," they trusted Him to lead them to safety. (Phil. 2:7-8) In practical terms, Matthew retells seven physical touch encounters, including several ceremonial untouchables.

COUNTERWEIGHTS

A counterweight is a weight that, by applying an opposite force, provides balance and stability of a mechanical system.[45]

There's a tendency here to overswing the dichotomy Christ's life presents to one extreme or the other. If we lean too heavily on the side of God's mercy, leaving aside His wrath or visa-versa, we only throw off the balance God has put in place. For example, if we wear mercy blinders and offer preferential treatment to the Lord as portrayed in Christmas hymns (i.e., "The babe in a manger, meek and mild, quietly wakes"), or to verses such as "Come to me, all of you who are weary and carry heavy burdens, and I will give you rest. Take my yoke upon you. Let me teach you, because I am *humble and gentle*

---

[44] *For 11 months out of every year Christianity is largely hidden from the public sector. Not December.*

[45] https://en.wikipedia.org/wiki/Counterweight

at heart,[46] we're left holding a half-finished product. The meek and mild have their place, no doubt. Jesus pronounced such people as being "blessed" in the Beatitudes. The Beatitudes were a series of "blessings" Jesus gave at the outset of His Sermon on the Mount. "Blessed are the poor in spirit, for theirs is the kingdom of heaven. Blessed are the gentle, for they shall inherit the earth. Blessed are the merciful, for they shall receive mercy."[47] That's not to be confused with being a pushover. If the Sermon on the Mount had volume, it began softly with the knob turned down low (Beatitudes) but cranked up to full blast by message end. It contains the sharpest edge of all Jesus' teachings. You can hear the counterbalance if you listen to it from start to finish.

- Do not give what is holy to dogs, and do not throw your pearls before swine![48]

- Every tree that does not bear good fruit is cut down and thrown into the fire.[49]

- I never knew you! Depart from Me you who practice lawlessness![50]

In the Chronicles of Narnia, a young girl named Lucy is curious about Aslan, a lion figure representing Christ. During her dialogue with Mr. And Mrs. Beaver, the latter cautions Lucy:

> "If there's anyone who can appear before Aslan without their knees knocking, they're either braver than most or else just silly," said Mrs. Beaver.

> "Then he isn't safe?" said Lucy.

---

[46] Matthew 11:28-29
[47] Matthew 5:3-7
[48] Matthew 7:6
[49] Matthew 7:19
[50] Matthew 7:23

"Safe?" said Mr. Beaver. "Don't you hear what Mrs. Beaver tells you? Who said anything about safe? 'Course he isn't safe. But he's good. He's the King, I tell you."[51]

Like Mr. and Mrs. Beaver, Philip Yancey posited, *"Jesus, I found, bore little resemblance to the Mister Roger's figure I had met in Sunday School, and was remarkably unlike the person I had studied in Bible college. For one thing, He was far less tame...Indeed, He seemed more emotional and spontaneous than the average person, not less. More passionate, not less."*[52] Would we agree that the church, or Christians, have tamed Christ? And if so, in what ways? In my opinion, we have. Like with Aslan the Lion, not Aslan the kitten, we need a healthy level of fear.

The Sermon on the Mount, at least from a micro perspective, exemplifies not only the Gospel as a whole but also, on a larger scale, the Old and New Testaments collectively. I say that because if you study all three chapters (5-7) in context, you'll notice how the spectrum's far ends of grace and truth temper each other. Theologians are quick to declare "grace and justice kiss in the person of Christ on the cross," which is undoubtedly true, not only for Scripture across the board, but for Matthew's Gospel as a whole, all the way down to this sermon. In sum, Mount Sinai's God is still present on the mountain, but far more tame.

GHIBERTI'S DOORS

Relief, also called relievo (from Italian relievare, "to raise"), in sculpture, is any work in which the figures project from a supporting background, usually a plane surface. Reliefs are classified according to the height of the figures' projection or detachment from the

---

[51] The Chronicles of Narnia: The Lion, The Witch, and the Wardrobe by C. S. Lewis
[52] Yancey, Philip. *The Jesus I Never Knew*

background. Lorenzo Ghiberti, an Italian sculptor and goldsmith of the Renaissance era (1378-1455 AD), was renowned for his mastery of relief work. Ghiberti's Bronze Doors of the Baptistery are situated in the cathedral of Florence. The iconic North Bronze doors highlight 28 panels that depict the life of Christ in the New Testament. The East gate, however, would become known as the most spectacular. These doors were comprised of 10 larger panels inspired by Old Testament heroes of faith. They were crafted over 27 years and stand approximately 17 feet tall. Michelangelo aptly referred to them as the 'Gates of Paradise,' a title that remains with them today. Ghiberti had the ability to cast some figures in the foreground in high relief, thus appearing close at hand, while background features were done in low relief, thus approximating distance.

In the same way, Matthew elevates Jesus far over and above the Biblical figures who proceeded Him (high relief) but manages to do so without blotting the others out (low relief). The New Covenant protrudes from the Old; it is not distinct from it. Much like Ghiberti's doors, Matthew's composition is a carefully crafted masterpiece that demonstrates the author's skill in the art of storytelling. It's a masterful display. We can see the blending the old and new.[53]

GRAFFITI

In second grade, I was not pegged as an artistic prodigy. Ghiberti and Michelangelo's positions remain safe. When the time came to hand out the 1974 grand end-of-school-year awards to each student, my teacher gave me the "Best with Scissors" award. This comes into stark contrast with the awards given to Beth Ann (Best Musician), Grant (Most Athletic), or Virginia (Best Painter by Numbers). Mrs. West clearly had to dig deep to find my hidden talent, which even I figured was a stretch considering how cruddy I was at cutting out things. I felt

---

[53] An interesting factoid, in 1419 Ghiberti won the commission to make a statue of Saint Matthew.

better suited for graffiti, a well-known fact my mother could attest to. She used her antique secretary for years. One day, while paying bills, with the sunlight shining from just the right angle, she made out as plain as day, "George Shamblin WUZ here," carved in cursive on the secretary. Years ago, she would have been furious. But as those years have gone by and faded into fond memories, so too has the carving faded. Putting down her pen, checkbook, and bills, she proceeded to the kitchen to find something to alleviate the problem of a faded signature on a highly valued possession. She didn't return with wood polish or finish, but with a sharp knife. She then began to re-carve out each letter, one by one, to safekeep a fond memory of her youngest child.

If the Old Testament conceals the New Testament and the New Testament reveals the Old, then both forever remain inseparably linked. Jesus claimed as much in Matthew 13:16-17, "But blessed are your eyes, because they see; and your ears, because they hear. For truly I say to you that many prophets and righteous men desired to see what you see, and did not see it, and to hear what you hear, and did not hear it." Matthew's telling didn't allow the Old Testament to fade away with the years. He included the colorful, timeless cast of characters, themes, and storylines. He re-carves each letter for us one by one, yet in the hue of the new covenant, to keep the original brilliance as before. Indeed, things are different now between the two testaments, but their harmony is undeniable. "At that time Jesus said, 'I praise You, Father, Lord of heaven and earth, that You have hidden these things from the wise and intelligent and have revealed them to infants. Yes, Father, for this way was well-pleasing in Your sight,'" (Matthew 11:25-26).

Through the power of the Holy Spirit, Matthew's recount has opened untold infants' hearts over the centuries. I never tire of hearing conversion accounts centered around this book. But the Gospel work doesn't stop there. Believers never arrive; we are to continually progress. And as we get enlightened more and more, our Savior certainly does appear to get bigger with each passing page.

I am reminded of a profound scene from C. S. Lewis' *Prince Caspian*. A long time has passed, and Lucy sees Aslan again after entering Narnia. This rich dialogue ensues:

> "'Aslan,' said Lucy, 'you're bigger.'
> 'That is because you are older, little one,' answered he.
> 'Not because you are?'
> 'I am not. But every year you grow, you will find me bigger.'"

That last sentence just strikes me. Here it is again with a few emphases and italics added: "I am not. <u>But</u> *every year* <u>*you grow*</u>, *you will find* <u>*Me bigger*</u>."

At the end of the day, studying this Gospel enlarges my concept of Jesus. It's not that He gets bigger; God is the same yesterday, today and forever. He just *appears* bigger, because I am able to see Him a little more as He truly is, which in turn causes me to grow.

Discussion Questions for "Matthew: What Do You Want Us to See?"

Look Back:

Share how you categorized your life if it were played out on center stage for others to see. Describe the cast of characters you foresaw and their order of prominence. Who or what stood out most? Who did you add behind the scenes that supports you?

Facing the Storms of Life:

1. How does the story of encountering the kitten before Hurricane Opal illustrate our response to fear and uncertainty in the midst of life's storms?

The Encounter at Mount Sinai:

2. Explore Exodus 19:16-19 and discuss the Israelites' reaction to encountering God on Mount Sinai. How does their fear and trembling contrast with our approach to Jesus as our Savior?

Encountering Jesus in the New Testament:

3. Reflect on Matthew 1:22-23 and how Jesus' arrival in the New Testament differs from the thunderous revelation at Mount Sinai. How does Jesus' incarnation demonstrate God's desire to relate to us on a personal level?

Balancing Grace and Truth:

4. It's important to maintain a balance between God's mercy and His justice. How does this balance shape our understanding of Jesus' character and mission?

The Sermon on the Mount:

5. How does the Sermon on the Mount (Matthew 5-7) embody both grace and truth, challenging us to live out a holistic faith? On a scale of 1-5, how would you rate your faith life's balance? Do you lean more to grace or to truth?

The Harmony of the Old and New Testaments:

6. In what ways does Matthew's Gospel bridge the gap between the Old and New Covenants, highlighting the continuity and harmony between them?

OLD TESTMENT		NEW TESTMENT
Law		*Grace*
Heroes of the Faith		*Jesus*
Prophets		

Personal Growth in Faith:

7. Re-read the quote from C. S. Lewis' Prince Caspian about Aslan appearing bigger as Lucy grows older. How does our understanding of Jesus deepen and expand as we grow in our faith journey?

8. Comment on the following: Would we agree that the church, or Christians, have tamed Christ? And if so, in what ways?

Action Step for Next Week:

As mentioned, Matthew retells seven physical touch encounters from Christ. Today's most marginalized segment of society are the elderly, who crave affectionate touch, especially those who reside in nursing homes. Set a time for your group to go visit the nearest nursing home. Don't delay! The administration has games and activities.

CHAPTER 6

What Do You Want Us to See, Mark?

"See but One Thing: The Son"

Many years ago, there was a very wealthy man who shared a passion for art collecting with his son. They had priceless works by Picasso and Van Gogh adorning the walls of their family estate. As winter approached, war engulfed the nation, and the young man left to serve his country. After only a few short weeks, his father received a telegram. His son had died. Distraught and lonely, the old man faced the upcoming Christmas holidays with anguish and sadness. The joy of the season had vanished with the death of his son. On Christmas morning, a knock on the door awakened the depressed old man. As he walked to the door, the masterpieces of art on the walls only reminded him that his son was not coming home. As he opened the door, he was greeted by a soldier with a large package in his hands who said, "I was a friend of your son. I was the one he was rescuing when he died. May I come in for a few moments? I have something to show you."

The soldier mentioned that he was an artist and then gave the old man the package. The paper gave way to reveal a portrait of the man's son. Though the world would never consider it the work of a genius, the painting featured the young man's face in striking detail. Overcome with emotion, the man hung the portrait over the fireplace, pushing aside millions of dollars' worth of art. With his task completed, the old man sat in his chair and spent Christmas gazing at the gift he had been given. The painting of his son soon became his most prized possession, far eclipsing any interest in the pieces of art for which museums around the world clamored.

The following spring, the old man died. The art world waited with anticipation for the upcoming auction. According to the will of the old man, all the art works would be auctioned on Christmas Day, the day he had received the greatest gift. The day soon arrived, and art collectors from around the world gathered to bid on some of the world's most spectacular paintings. Dreams would be fulfilled that day. The auction began with a painting that was not on anyone's museum list. It was the painting of the man's son. The auctioneer asked for an opening bid, but the room was silent. "Who will open the bidding with $100?" No one spoke. Eventually, someone said, "Who cares about that painting. It's just a picture of his son. Let's move on to the good stuff." The auctioneer responded, "No, we have to sell this one first. Now, who will take the son?" Finally, a neighbor of the old man offered $10. "That's all I have. I knew the boy, so I'd like to have it." The auctioneer said, "Going once, going twice...gone." The gavel fell. Cheers filled the room and someone exclaimed, "Now we can bid on the real treasures!" The auctioneer looked at the room filled with people and announced that the auction was over. Everyone was stunned. Someone spoke up and said, "What do you mean, it's over? We didn't come here for a painting of someone's son. There are millions of dollars' worth of art here! What's going on?" The auctioneer replied, "It's very simple. According to the will of the father, whoever gets the son...gets it all." It puts things in perspective, doesn't it? The message is the same every Christmas. Because of the Father's love... whoever gets the Son gets it all.

Had Mark been an artist, I would not assign him to the list of greats such as Rembrandt, Raphael, or Monet. His finishing touches aren't as pristine as Luke's. Whereas Luke's Greek was polished and more refined, Mark was a blue-collar, paint-by-numbers kind of guy. His sentences are fragmented, his thought processes get choppy, and his arrangement of material is crude. For him, the meat and potatoes of the Good News were at issue. The finer details, or nuances, only slowed him down. Do not misunderstand; by no means am I suggesting his rendition held less intrinsic value, far from it. It's just rudimentary, comparable to refrigerator artwork. And if you were to ask any parent or grandparent, "Is anything on earth more precious in your sight than your child's artwork taped to the refrigerator? Like Picasso? Or Van Gogh?" Not a chance; in the eye of the beholder, they're equally priceless.

Mark, analogous to the soldier and his portrait from the story above, makes one thing clear—whoever gets the Son gets it all. It's Jesus alone that we must see and consider. But he lets on that we're not supposed to remain stationary forever, deliberating over what we see (like patrons at museums musing at stills for hours on end). We gather that Mark's sights are set way ahead, like down a path or trail he's pushing us towards.

If we pretend to be first-time readers, we can picture him walking while talking nervously, filling us in on pertinent details, and catching us up to speed as we travel. Every 5-10 steps, he steadily peers back over his shoulder to ensure we're still attentive while rushing ahead and waving his hand ever so often in a circular motion, directing us to keep up the pace and not lag too far behind. He's dying to get us somewhere quickly, but where? I promise we will arrive there eventually, but many matters must be attended to first.

IMMEDIATELY!

Mark's portrayal is action-packed, like a high-speed chase on television. He employs two stand-out words, "immediately" and "and." "Immediately" appears a whopping 41 times! Its purpose is to keep us on pace with the scurry of events surrounding Jesus. For instance:

- "*Immediately* the Spirit impelled Him to go out into the wilderness." (Mk. 1:12)

- "They *immediately* left their nets and followed Him." (Mk. 1:18)

- "The Pharisees went out and *immediately* began conspiring with the Herodians against Him." (Mk. 3:6)

- Taking the child by the hand, He said to her, 'Little girl, I say to you, get up!' *Immediately* the girl got up and began to walk, for she was twelve years old. And *immediately* they were completely astounded." (Mk. 5:41-42)

The mission moves. It's in constant motion, and we can see it vividly.

AND!

And if the casual reader feels a pause is in order between the 41 "immediatelies" to stop and take a breather, that's not happening. The "ands" that connect the chapters together disallow it. This is what I mean. After the narrative begins (i.e., "The beginning of the gospel of Jesus Christ, the Son of God"),[54] every subsequent chapter (except 8 and 14) starts with "and." The function of "and" in literature is "to connect more than two elements together in a chain." So, let's say you finish reading chapter one. Before you get to chapter two, you're immediately met by the conjunction "and." It's like a chain of events is established, and it cannot be stopped:

> "Jesus could no longer publicly enter a city, but stayed out in unpopulated areas; and they were coming to Him from everywhere **AND** when He had come back to Capernaum several days afterward, it was heard that He was at home."

The above demonstrates how "AND" connects chapter one's last verse with chapter two's first verse (Mark 1:45-2:1). The transition is seamless. Although you won't see it in most translations, it's in the

---

[54] Mark 1:1

---

original Greek. Clearly, Mark's intent is to get us somewhere fast. We're left to wonder, where?

GRAECO-ROMAN TRAVEL GUIDE

One more significant observation needs to be made before traveling farther. If we were to pretend Mark is a tour guide in the Holy Land (antsy as ever), he's not going to give every tourist the same pre-packaged spiel. Instead, he will customize his presentation to meet *that* particular crowd where *they are* and as *they* are. More specifically, his target audience is predominately Greeks within the Roman Empire.

How is that determined? We know Mark was partial towards non-Jews or Greeks and wrote primarily to them, given several clues. First, Mark's account isn't devoid of Old Testament references, but he only uses them sparingly. The Torah may have been the lifeblood of Judaism, but it carried little weight beyond its borders. Secondly, Mark went out of his way to unpack customs that were familiar to every Jew (like washings and purifications) but were totally foreign concepts to everyone else (Greeks).

Picture it this way: if two Americans were discussing plans for Thanksgiving, there would be no reason for either to define the tradition, describe its origins, or explain why it's celebrated. Turkey and dressing, the Detroit Lions, the Dallas Cowboys, fall, leaves, pumpkins, and a celebration of the harvest, are all a given. If, on the other hand, either of them mentioned Thanksgiving to a non-citizen, each aspect of the holiday would require further explanation. In the same way, when the contentious subject arose over ceremonial cleansing in chapter seven, Mark had to frame it in a non-Jewish context. Notice how "they" occurs six times in italics.

> 1The Pharisees and some of the scribes gathered around Him when *they* had come from Jerusalem, 2and had seen that some of His

disciples were eating their bread with impure hands, that is, unwashed. 3(For the Pharisees and all the Jews do not eat unless _they_ carefully wash their hands, thus observing the traditions of the elders; 4and when _they_ come from the market place, _they_ do not eat unless _they_ cleanse themselves; and there are many other things which _they_ have received in order to observe, such as the washing of cups and pitchers and copper pots.)[55]

What's more, preparations on Friday in advance of the Sabbath were commonplace even among Palestine's least observant Jews. But this audience required further explanation, implying once again that they weren't Jewish. "When evening had already come, because it was the preparation day, _that is, the day before the Sabbath_, Joseph of Arimathea came…and asked for the body of Jesus."[56]

UNLIKE YOUR GODS

Given this target audience, in what light is the controversial Nazarene cast? If you studied world history at school, you might recall how Greek and Romans mindsets were pre-set to the Pantheons of gods and goddesses. The Roman Empire was polytheistic, meaning its citizens worshipped multiple gods. On the front end of his exposition, Mark borrowed verbiage familiar to all Romans, i.e., "sons of the gods," to garner their interest-not like a bait and switch, but more of a lure and set the hook, if we can borrow fishermen's terms. But Mark then added one vital differentiator: Christ was not _a son of the gods_ but _The Son of God_! Not only could Gentiles identify with this initially, they could rest assured that an audience with the Ruler of Creation was available to all. Mark inserts Son of God references at the beginning, middle, and end of his narration to reinforce that point:

---

[55] Mark 7:1-4
[56] Mark 15:42-43

- **Beginning** - "The gospel of Jesus Christ, *the Son of God*." (Mk. 1:1)

- **Middle** - A demon-possessed man "seeing Jesus from a distance, he ran up and bowed down before Him; and shouting with a loud voice, he said, 'What business do we have with each other, Jesus, *Son of the Most High God*?'" (Mk. 5:6-7)

- **End** - "When the centurion, who was standing right in front of Him, saw the way He breathed His last, he said, 'Truly this man was *the Son of God*!'"[57] (Mk. 15:39)

BITTER MOLASSES

After reaching the summit, I've often wondered what "the letdown effect" must feel like to a mountain climber. Victory is forever vulnerable to letdown. "When you get to the peak, remember the valley exists." - Ernest Agyemang Yeboah

To go back to our travails with Mark, I do know that sense of accomplishment is incomplete because the expedition isn't over. In the same manner, Mark 10:32 is like a summit for us. We can catch our breath for the first time since departure while resting off the brow, overlooking Jerusalem from the east. But we're far from finished. Everything's about to change on a dime from this point forward. Mark 10:32 is a hinge verse where the narrative's pace slows drastically, almost to a molasses-like crawl. We've been hurried up to wait.

> "Now they were on the road going up to Jerusalem, and Jesus was walking on ahead of them; and they were amazed, and those who followed were fearful. And again He took the twelve aside and began to tell them what was going to happen to Him." (Mk. 10:32)

---

[57] Mark was wise to use such a credible source (a roman soldier) to validate Christ.

We no longer have to wonder where Mark wants to get us so fast. This is it. We're here! Jerusalem! Notice where Jesus's sites are set for these final travels—Jerusalem, a city to be wept over for not realizing the time of its visitation: "Oh Jerusalem, Jerusalem, who kills the prophets and stones those who are sent to her! How often I wanted to gather your children together, the way a hen gathers her chicks under her wings, and you were unwilling."[58] Our tour guide, Mark, spared no details as we bore down upon the city's outer limits. He walks slower and talks slower and more methodically than before. He's careful to point out noteworthy tidbits and insights between each step. In fact, around 40% of his material is dedicated to Jesus' final week on earth! Stated differently, it takes roughly 10 chapters to cover 33 years of Christ's life and 6 and ½ chapters to cover the last seven days.

In particular, there's something major he won't allow his readership to miss: the criminal's crosses that loom ahead. It's as if Mark pleads with us, "Whatever it takes, I will not allow you to miss that middle cross!" Mark partitions us off to the distance somewhat cruelly, albeit effectively. We are close enough to observe the events as they unfold but too far away to sway the predetermined outcome. The site, sound, smell, and heavy weightiness of atoning death are far away but close-a midway point between one's senses and imagination.

PRECURSOR OF WRATH TO COME

Throughout the myriads of stops and starts, ascending and descending, traveling up and traveling down, running fast to get there only to slow down once we arrive, we've solidified Mark's primary aim: The Son of God's atonement on the cross. But now that we're at the trials' end (at least for now), I want you to notice what remains unresolved. **This is a major, major issue we have yet to grapple with**. Seriously, please take a moment to think about it. Is there something

---

[58] Matthew 23:37

else Mark wants us to see and consider? Could a lesser cross with your initials be relegated to the shadows?

Consider what happened to John the Baptist, the most remarkable man who ever lived according to Jesus, and how his head was presented to King Herod on a platter. And if we recall what happened to God's Son—betrayals, false accusations, whippings, mock trials, executioners (I hope you follow where this is going), we must undoubtedly ask: What, then, will happen to us, His followers? If our mission is to be a continuation of His mission, how's that supposed to play out? When Jesus extended His hand while proclaiming, "Go into all the world and preach the gospel to all creation"[59] did the scars on His palms register with the disciples? Should we imply that His scars will become our scars? Could Dietrich Bonhoeffer be right? "When Christ calls a man, He bids him 'come and die.'" Given the above, I think the answer is "quite possibly."

I find it incredibly curious that the earliest artwork on record pertaining to Christianity is Alexandro's Graffito in the 1st century. This "graffito," representing a person looking at a donkey-headed man being crucified, was carved in plaster on a wall in Rome during

The author is providing the above image for clarity but does not condone creating mockeries of Christ in real life.

[59] Mark 16:15

the 1st century. If you feel confused or offended by its content, it was not created as a celebration of Jesus but rather as a mockery.

During the 1st century, Christianity was not an official religion, and most Roman citizens looked at its practitioners with suspicion and skepticism. This graffiti was probably created to make fun of "Alexandros," a Christian, by implying that he worshiped a "donkey-headed" God. The inscription accompanying the image reads, "Alexandro worshiping his god." The fact that "Alexandro's God" is being crucified makes it even worse, as during the 1st century, crucifixion was a punishment reserved for serious crime offenders.

Add to this artwork an ominous warning from Jesus of Nazareth to would-be followers in the thick of Mark's Gospel: "If anyone wishes to come after Me, he must deny himself, and *take up his cross* and follow Me. For whoever wishes to save his life will lose it, but whoever loses his life for My sake and the gospel's will save it" (Mark 8:34-35). The only individuals in 1st Century Palestine taking up crosses and carrying them were headed to death; a brutal fact noted by all.

In Mark 13:11, Jesus foresaw the day not **if** they arrest you and hand you over, but "**when** they arrest you and hand you over." Do we live in a time when warnings should be heeded more than before? Does Mark come out and say it? Maybe not explicitly, but the implication definitely lingers. I am convinced that Mark gives us a heads-up about what we're signing up for. No fine print. No legal disclaimers. Discipleship comes with a price tag and a cost. Rather than answering the question outright, "Mark, what do you want us to see?" do you suppose he wants us to walk away asking, "What price am I willing to pay?"

Discussion Questions for "Mark, What Do You Want Us to See?"

Look Back:

Was your group able to serve a local Nursing Home or get a date set on the calendar?

Reflection on Loss and Redemption:

1. How does the story of the wealthy man and his son resonate with you?

Comparison of Artistic Styles:

2. What do you think the author means by describing Mark's writing as "rudimentary" but equally priceless, akin to a child's artwork?

3. In the eyes of God, how can our good works be comparable to a kid's refrigerator artwork?

Audience Consideration:

4. How does understanding Mark's target audience, primarily Greek and Roman, influence our interpretation of his Gospel?

The Identity of Jesus:

5. Discuss the implications of referring to Jesus as "the Son of God" in a cultural context where the term was often associated with pagan deities.

Journey to Jerusalem:

6. How does the narrative slow down and become more deliberate as Jesus approaches Jerusalem? What emotions and tensions are conveyed in this transition?

The Cross and Discipleship:

7. What does Jesus' call to discipleship, including the command to take up one's cross, mean in the context of Mark's Gospel and for contemporary believers?

Persecution and Martyrdom:

8. Reflect on the theme of martyrdom in the context of Mark's Gospel. How does the example of Jesus and His followers challenge our understanding of discipleship and sacrifice?

9. In what sense could a lesser cross with your initials be relegated to the shadows?

Art and Mockery:

10. How does Alexandro's *Graffito* reflect the cultural and religious context of the first-century Roman Empire? What type of artwork might typify culture's perceptions of Christianity today?

11. What price are you willing to pay to follow Jesus, considering the themes of sacrifice, persecution, and redemption presented in Mark's Gospel?

Action Step for Next Week:

Get uncomfortable. Visit a place where you'll engage with non-believers, and feel the weight of following Christ. You could go to a secular book club, or non-Christian religious festival, have dinner with unbelieving coworkers after work, or meet with an unbelieving family member.

CHAPTER 7

What Do You Want Us to See, Luke?

"See People for Who They are in Christ, Not for Who They Were Without Him"

DADDY WOUNDS

Druid City Hospital's endless mazes of hallways, stairwells, cafeterias, elevators, lounges, waiting rooms, and parking garages begged for us doctor's kids from the Highlands to run crazy. They seemed endless, larger than life. It wasn't possible for us to quietly ease into a game of chase or subtly slip into playing hide and seek under the radar. As such, had timers been set for the amount of time it took for us to get kicked out, it'd register anywhere between 15 and 30 minutes, tops. The adult in charge always demanded names be given whenever we got caught. As soon as I let on who I was, "Which Shamblin are you?" became a predictable reply. Thirteen physicians sharing the same last name in a college town make for standing out. "I'm Bill's son." I wore it as a badge of honor then and continued to do so until I turned fifteen. That's when the wheels fell off.

My family fell to pieces when I was 15 years old, during my freshman year of high school. Going into details is unnecessary because all is forgiven. Suffice it to say, there were a lot of poor decisions made in public on my dad's part. I can tell you that what I once wore as a badge of honor, "Which Shamblin are you?" turned into a term of derision and shame. I recall giving the same reply every time: "That's not who I am. I am my own man." It still kind of makes me sad thinking how pitiful it was trying to be tough and strong by saying "I am my own man," although I was just a kid. I tell you, I was one wounded soul.

Brokenness is: Humpty Dumpty, who had a great fall, and all the king's horses and all the king's men couldn't put Humpty together again.

"I don't work with college kids who have daddy wounds," a college pastor casually assured a group of us ministers at a conference in 2021, trying to be cool. "Well," I curtly retorted, "has anyone informed you you're in the wrong profession, dude?" What an idiotic thing to think, much less say aloud, especially for a man whose job is tending to wounded sheep on campus. "*Those who are sickly you have not strengthened, the diseased you have not healed, the broken you have not bound up, the scattered you have not brought back, nor have you searched for the lost*" (Ez. 34:4). Daddy wounds cut deep, as profoundly as a soul's wounds can go. This is an excellent point to remind us to cut others slack; you never know the hurt someone is going through.

HER REASON FOR LOVING MUCH

Never, ever, ever think that miracles no longer happen. Never. They certainly do—supernatural ones. In fact, I have had a rather dramatic experience myself. The change wrought over me at La Paz Restaurant in the winter of 1993 was miraculous.

I had committed my life to Christ three months earlier, in October 1992. In one of his letters, Paul refers to the need to "put off the old man."[60] The old George was putting up one heck of a fight, meaning

---

[60] Ephesians 4:22-24

the resentment I held towards my father lingered like the stench a dead fish leaves behind long after you throw it out. No matter how hard I tried to shake it, I couldn't. It is impossible to try and articulate how much I loathed him; it simply cannot be put into words. I'm embarrassed and ashamed to admit it now, but many readers likely relate to what I mean.

My wife, Jill, and I were enjoying dinner at La Paz in Birmingham, Alabama. I must have elaborated on my conversion because something triggered Jill to lean over the table to say, "What are you going to do about your dad?" I knew why she asked; bitterness is like drinking poison, hoping for another to die.

As I stared through the window, I could see the cars driving down the road in a misty rain and hear the swooshing tire sounds of each as they passed by. Within two minutes, two stark realizations struck me. (Don't ask how I vividly recall it being two minutes; I just do because it was so monumental.) First, practically, as a new creation in Christ, I didn't want my dad to exert power over me anymore. By clinging to the bitterness, I relinquished control, and the last thing I wanted was for him to control me. Second, this story from Luke 7 flashed across my mind:

> 40And Jesus responded and said to him, "Simon, I have something to say to you." And he replied, "Say it, Teacher." 41"A moneylender had two debtors: the one owed five hundred denarii, and the other, fifty. 42When they were unable to repay, he canceled the debts of both. So which of them will love him more?" 43Simon answered and said, "I assume the one for whom he canceled the greater debt." And He said to him, "You have judged correctly." 44And turning toward the woman, He said to Simon, "Do you see this woman? I entered your house; you gave Me no water for My feet, but she has wet My feet with her tears and wiped them with her hair. 45You gave Me no kiss; but she has not stopped kissing

> My feet since the time I came in. 46You did not
> anoint My head with oil, but she anointed My feet
> with perfume. 47For this reason I say to you, her sins,
> which are many, have been forgiven, for she loved
> much; but the one who is forgiven little, loves little."

This story *is* my conversion. They are one and the same. I relate to this woman of ill repute more than anyone in Scripture. I could have been her from the moment I first said "yes" to the Gospel. I collapsed straight to my knees; if only His physical feet had been before me, I'd have wept uncontrollably over them. Had I any oil, I'd pour the last drop on His feet as a love offering to my Savior. All the while, I was desperately wanting to scream out, "Why would you possibly save me? You know what I've done. Why me?"[61]

I rationalized that my debt, which was more than 500 denarii, had been forgiven. This gave me a greater capacity to love much. How could I refuse forgiveness to someone like my dad, whose debt was less than 50 denarii? Turning away from the windowsill of cars driving by in misty rain, I said, **"That's it. It's gone. *It's over.*"** By the power of the Holy Spirit, who does "far more abundantly beyond all that we ask or think, according to the power that works within us,"[62] all 1,000+ pounds of burden lifted off my back in 120 seconds. I'd released it. I'd released him, and both parties were forever free.

How was I sure it was gone? Excitedly, I drove to meet my dad the following morning to tell him the good news: "I forgive you!" His reply? "What have I ever done that needs forgiveness?" It was like water off a duck's back. I looked upon my father with genuine love

---

[61] Incredibly, the same setting for my top illustration on sin can be found at the same location of everything else in this chapter: Druid City Hospital. sin is—as defined by a sign I saw over the parking garage at Druid City Hospital in Tuscaloosa, Alabama— "Free In, Pay Out." It doesn't cost anything to get in. But you have to pay to get out. As the saying goes, "Sin will take you farther than you want to go, keep you longer than you want to stay, and cost you more than you want to pay."

[62] Ephesians 3:20

and compassion like never before, proof positive that a miracle had indeed occurred.

Since then, I have tried to do what Luke wants us to do: see people for who they are in Christ, not for who they were without Him. Or, in cases of people who don't know the Lord, let's give the benefit of "not yet."

> And Levi gave a big reception for Him in his house; and there was a great crowd of tax collectors and other people who were reclining at the table with them. 30The Pharisees and their scribes began grumbling at His disciples, saying, "Why do you eat and drink with the tax collectors and sinners?" 31And Jesus answered and said to them, "It is not those who are well who need a physician, but those who are sick. 32I have not come to call the righteous but sinners to repentance." (Luke 5:29-32)

I imagine that many of you will relate to this piece on bitterness more than the rest of the book. I hope so. If I can be practical here for a moment, let's consider the person who wounded you deeply and who cut you in the place where it hurt most. Like a movie reel continuously playing in your head, you assure yourself, "I have a right to be mad at them. It was shameful what they did. They don't deserve to be forgiven! They haven't asked for forgiveness." Let's assume these feelings are valid. Is that the type of standard Jesus set for you? No. His is much higher, and you fell more woefully short. And yet, where do you find yourself now? "When they could not repay, he canceled the debts of both" (Luke 7:42). Please let that gently remind you.

YOUR PATIENTS WILL BE THE FIRST TO KNOW

But oh, how the Lord can take a bitter story and bring it full circle to make it right. If Part 1 of the narrative speaks to the power of forgiveness, Part 2 speaks to all things restoration.

How cool is it that ten years later, when I was 25, in the same childhood maze I ran around as a 15-year-old, Jesus sewed together a series of events that plopped me right back into the thick of Druid City Hospital alongside my dad! Within a nine-hour workday in the fall of 1995, I saw layers peel back that I'd never witnessed. It's what made all the difference, then as well as now. Water had passed so far under the bridge that it had long since dissipated at sea. And at the center of it all was the difference between a medical doctor and a physician and a precious parable in Luke.

When I became a sales rep with Merck and Company, I had the satisfaction of calling on dozens of physicians throughout my territory who'd done medical school rotations under my father. Cutting, sewing, and making rounds weren't art forms per se. Precision and attention to detail, yes, are skills necessary in the operating room, obviously. Still, scalpels in the hands of one practitioner can't be too dissimilar from a scalpel in another. Not so, according to these doctors. They universally agreed that he possessed extraordinary surgical ability. Yet nobody could articulate precisely what it was. So, what in the world was it?

From a purely professional level, could it have been his credentials? Those indeed were impeccable. Four-year residency at Ochsner Clinic. Two-year fellowship at the Mayo Clinic. Staff Surgeon at the Mayo Clinic. He was double board certified in general surgery and vascular surgery, hospital chief of staff, medical school professor, and so on. None of this particularly impressed me or my siblings growing up, other than noticing how goofy it caused medical personnel (and practically every community member) to act in his company. Be that as it may, credentials didn't unravel the mystery.

The answer to that question came in a surprising form: a preceptorship required by Merck & Co. Each representative had to shadow a surgeon in their territory; my father became the obvious choice. Not only did I get scrubbed up to see him in action in the operating room, but I also had the double privilege of making rounds by his side. Before we continue, let me point out that this was the pre-boomer generation known for embracing their kids like wooden 2x4s. "Hugs" were doled out in a sterile, clinical fashion. They were never full-on frontal hugs, but side-to-side, every single time. They were often accompanied by his obligatory two pats on the back (again, like a 2x4), the antithesis of warm, affectionate, and fuzzy. Not so with his patients, though; his became a comforting touch, a calming and commanding demeanor that altered the air as soon as his feet brushed over the threshold. It surprised me. I've never physically felt a room change like that day. It caught me completely off guard to see him lean over a diabetic lady's hospital bed, patting his hand softly on top of hers, leaning in to listen to her barely audible, labored words. It was so touching to experience him extending deep compassion from deep within to sick and desperate souls. I remember thinking it was easier for him, perhaps not knowing them intimately or socially.

Anyways, we had developed a bond during those days. We were living out in real-time, verses like Joel 2:24-25. After enduring years of famine and crop devastation, the Israelites were hopeful of a day coming soon: "The threshing floors will be full of grain, and the vats will overflow with the new wine and oil. *Then I will make up to you* for the years that the swarming locust has eaten." I'll confess. That same afternoon, while strolling the hospital's halls, I have never heard more impressionable words than when my dad leaned my way to whisper, "I'm proud of you, George." It was a first, and he meant it. I'm confident he did.

Since then, I've had time to reminisce, wildly curious about what had transpired. My father passed away in 2003, and this is the conclusion I came up with. He'd officially graduated and received medical degrees by completing all the necessary coursework. Beginning in 1965, such licensure had changed his name; it grew longer. He no longer went by William Shamblin, but *Dr.* William R. Shamblin, *M.D.*

But you know what? Somewhere along the way, something new had transpired at a precise point; he'd undergone a metamorphosis. A genuine bedside manner had crept in for the first time, and boy, did it creep in ever so deeply. No longer was he merely a clinician, but he'd grown into a full-fledged physician, with the love, care, and compassion for those entrusted to his care. Not dissimilar to Luke, the beloved Physician. It's doubtful he ever noticed how or when that transformation occurred, but I assure you, others did. I may have been a latecomer to recognize it. But not his patients; they, the patients, are always the first to know.

So, looking back, how do I see my dad? Very positively. I once heard a kid say, "Everybody's a 10 at something," and you know what? He's right. My father left behind a large stack of things he was a 10 at, all of which I am beyond grateful for.

JARS OF CLAY

Luke's narration, rushes me back to an indelible image from 1992 or so while driving to a wedding way out in the country. For the life of me, I can't recall the nearest town, church, or even the couple, for that matter. The strangeness of what transpired during the ceremony is all that stood out.

The sanctuary's stage, where I presumed the bride and groom would shortly ascend to exchange vows, was entirely void of all the pomp and circumstance that usually accompanies most weddings. Save the podium illumined under a single, beaming spotlight: plain, not fancy, undecorated, and oblique. Not so much as a laced ribbon or a blossoming flower donned a thing, unlike any other wedding my mother dragged me to. Stranger still was the ugliest centerpiece imaginable occupying the top of that podium: a filthy, muddy, unsculptured chunk of dirty clay for all to see.

A middle-aged man wearing all black slipped onto the stage to remove the awful eyesore (a custodian, I presumed). But why was he carrying a satchel of tools? That's when he immediately set about crafting his trade. Within a minute, it became apparent that he was a potter sculpting something from clay. Three minutes in, still no groom or bride had been seen. The pile of shavings mounting up on the floor caught my eye. I fixated on them almost like in a fog: "Who gets to clean that mess up?" passed through my mind. By the time I looked up, the bust of a man had emerged.

The artist, whose hands had been flinging with mud, momentarily stepped back like a judge gauging his progress. That's when I saw it, or saw Him, you could say. How fascinating that an artist could twist and contort clay in such a way to make prickly thorns protrude from One's brow! "How cruel," it felt, "for a King to be coronated by such an unbecoming crown." Halos are the better fit.

Looking down further, strikes, stripes, and streaks of agony adorned His face. What degree of artistic flare would it take to leave the impression that screams could be heard if only we would listen? A preposterous notion that a clay mold could speak! It felt as if He could.

The clay had been clay all along, but when crafted under the watchful eye of the sculptor, it made all the difference. So it is with us, imaged in the likeness of Christ. "But now, LORD, You are our Father; We are the clay, and You our potter, And all of us are the work of Your hand" (Isaiah 64:8).

If ever I'm tempted to look down on someone else, it behooves me to revisit that small-town sanctuary and remember what happened there. Even a fool like Job's friend Elihu made a wise connection: "Behold, I belong to God, like you; I too have been formed out of the clay."[63] Peering behind my shoulder over the course of a lifetime what do I see? Not a clinician, but thanks to Luke, a physician.

---

[63] Job 33:6

Discussion Questions for "Luke, What Do You Want Us to See?"

Look Back:

Were you able to enter an uncomfortable setting? What type of engagement came about while you were there? What did you learn about bearing your cross to follow Christ?

Forgiveness and Bitterness:

1. Share with the group a time you allowed bitterness to get a foothold and the harmful influence it had on your life.

2. Have you undergone a similar transformation resulting from forgiveness in your own life? If so, describe the circumstances.

3. In Luke 7:40-47, Jesus speaks about the forgiveness of debts and the depth of love that follows. How does this story relate to a Christian's journey of forgiveness?

Restoration and Healing:

4. Reflect on the author's experience of hearing his father say, "I'm proud of you." How does affirmation and encouragement play a role in restoration?

5. What were some of the most life-giving words you've ever heard and from whom? Why was it so memorable?

Identity and Purpose:

6.   The author talks about his transition from wearing his father's name as a badge of honor to finding his own identity. How does this journey relate to finding one's identity in Christ?

7.   In Isaiah 64:8, the analogy of God as the potter and humans as the clay is used. How does this imagery inform our understanding of identity and purpose?

Compassion and Empathy:

8.   What can we learn about compassion from Jesus' interactions with others?

Miracles and Transformation:

9.   The author describes his experience of a miraculous transformation in his attitude towards his father. Have you ever witnessed or experienced a similar transformation in your own life or the life of someone you know?

10. Reflect on the role of miracles in the broader context of Christian faith. How do miracles point to the transformative power of God's love and grace?

Action Step for Next Week:

Write the initials of someone you're having a hard time forgiving on a piece of paper. Wad it up and carry in your pocket all week. Each time it reminds you of that person pray for restoration and claim Luke 18:27: "The things that are impossible with people are possible with God."

CHAPTER 8

What Do You Want Us to See, John?

"See and Believe"

Two men, both seriously ill, occupied the same small hospital room. One man was allowed to sit up in his bed for an hour each afternoon to help drain the fluid from his lungs. His bed was next to the room's only window. The other man had to spend all his time flat on his back. The men talked for hours on end. They spoke of their wives and families, their homes, their jobs, their involvement in the military service, and where they had been on vacation.

And every afternoon, when the man in the bed by the window could sit up, he would pass the time by describing to his roommate all the things he could see outside the window. The man in the other bed began to live for those one-hour periods where his world would be broadened and enlivened by all the activity and color of the outside world.

The window overlooked a park with a lovely lake, the man said. Ducks and swans played on the water while children sailed their model boats. Lovers walked arm in arm amid flowers of every color of the rainbow. Grand old trees graced the landscape, and a fine view of the city could be seen in the distance.

As the man by the window described all this in exquisite detail, the man on the other side of the room would close his eyes and imagine the picturesque scene.

One warm afternoon, the man by the window described a parade passing by. Although the other man couldn't hear the band - he could see it in his mind's eye as the gentleman by the window portrayed it with descriptive words.

Days and weeks passed.

One morning, the day nurse arrived to bring water for their baths only to find the lifeless body of the man by the window, who had died peacefully in his sleep. She was saddened and called the hospital attendants to take the body away. As soon as it seemed appropriate, the other man asked if he could be moved next to the window. The nurse was happy to make the switch, and after making sure he was comfortable, she left him alone.

Slowly, painfully, he propped himself up on one elbow to take his first look at the world outside. Finally, he would have the joy of seeing it for himself. He strained to look out the window beside the bed. It faced a blank wall.

The man asked the nurse what could have compelled his deceased roommate who had described such wonderful things outside this window. The nurse responded that the man was blind and could not even see the wall. She said, "Perhaps he just wanted to give you hope." (Target, G.W., *The Window*)

C an you imagine how challenging it would be to try and describe what the world's most exquisite rose, the Double Delight, looks like to someone who cannot see? How would you convey its complex design, or detail how its lush red and white petals merge perfectly at the stem? Not even its award-winning fragrance could assist you; aromas only appeal to the sense of smell, not sight. Or, how might you portray that same rose to a baby in the womb?

How daunting, therefore, the task must have been for John to relay what his experience with Christ looked like while Jesus was on earth. The closest description I can find comes from 1st John 1:1: "What was from the beginning, what we have heard, what we have seen with our eyes, what we have looked at and touched with our hands, concerning the Word of Life—and the life was manifested, and we have seen and testify and proclaim to you the eternal life, which was with the Father and was manifested to us—what we have seen and heard we proclaim to you also, so that you too may have fellowship with us; and indeed our fellowship is with the Father, and with His Son Jesus Christ."

Harder still was John's commission to share with others what heaven actually looks like in the Book of Revelation. Unlike anyone before or since, John peered behind the veil, witnessing a nether world known only by the dead. Transcribing "what is to come" was no less arduous than describing a rose's exquisite beauty to someone blind from birth. Had we been left with our own perceptions of heaven, much like the second man in the story above, we would mostly stare at a blank wall. But thanks to the illuminating power of the Holy Spirit, John not only gives posterity much-needed hope but also provides a pathway that we too may "see and believe,"[64] which was his reaction upon entering the empty tomb. In the minds of countless theologians, it is understandable why John's exposition is synonymous with "a Gospel of belief."

---

[64] John 20:8 "So the other disciple who had first come to the tomb then also entered, and he saw and believed."

The question has yet to be determined: what exactly did John want us to see? Evidently, according to his own reckoning, entire storehouses bursting at the seams of pertinent information about the life and ministry of Jesus of Nazareth were available to him. It was his call (by the leading of the Holy Spirit) to decide which resources to draw from when drafting his story for us. At the end of the day, or by the close of John's last verse, 21:25, he was intent on pulling out only that material most likely to highlight Christ, a more challenging proposition than you may think.

To set this up, let me begin with a comparison and contrast. I'll share two animal stories, starting with my two dachshunds, Mr. Franks and Otie, first. Those dogs are obsessed with chasing squirrels and chipmunks. It's the highlight of each day. Not once in a thousand attempts have they come close to being successful, but they won't give up. The far-right corner of my backyard is a meeting place for varmints. Literally holding my doggies up, they'd press their long snouts close to the windowsill. Like a hype song blaring before sporting events, I'd shake and rattle, yelling, "Go getcha squirrel, go getcha squirrel." With that, I'd be ready to spring the door wide open; Mr. Franks, the slower and little-legged of the two, stepped back initially to get a running start. Of the thousands of vain attempts at catching a squirrel, they flew off the back steps and took off, running left a thousand times. In every single instance, they saw that the action was to the right. But they ran left for whatever reason.

The second story is centered around a kennel trainer who was training lab puppies in the Mississippi Delta. The flooded rice fields and a plethora of ducks provided an ideal setting. One mid-morning, the trainer loaded up 14 lab pups. After an hour of drills, he loaded the pups back up and returned to camp. It wasn't until after lunch, five hours after morning drills, that he discovered one puppy was missing. Panicked, he sped off to the rice field as quickly as possible. Once he arrived, the lab pup was at the exact spot where she'd been left. She was still on point, unmoved, and unfazed by the sequence of events, including being left alone to fend for herself! Needless to say, the fact she never broke point elevated her to the pride of the pack, increasing her worth from $4,000 at sunset that day to $16,000 by sundown. A sizable profit for sure, but more importantly, she earned the adoration and favor of her master.

If you take a minute to peruse through John, it's impossible to miss how consistently everyone misses Jesus, not unlike Mr. Franks and Otie habitually breaking left instead of right. Look for yourself... It's everywhere. Everyone looks over Him, past Him, beyond Him, or even down on Him. Not once will you find an individual who first encounters Jesus and *sees Him*, and I mean *really sees Him* for Who He is, as in "with eyes to see"[65]. It takes a while for most, some longer than others; it's a progression.

- "Surely the Christ is not going to come from Galilee, is He?" (Jn. 7:41)

- "Search, and see that no prophet arises out of Galilee." (Jn. 7:52)

- "You are testifying about Yourself; Your testimony is not true." (Jn. 8:13)

- "Surely He will not kill Himself, will He?" (Jn. 8:22)

- "Surely You are not greater than our father Abraham, who died?" (Jn. 8:53)

- "How long will You keep us in suspense? If You are the Christ, tell us plainly." (Jn. 10:24)

- "Are You the King of the Jews?" (Jn. 18:33)

---

[65] "Hear this, O foolish and senseless people, who have eyes but do not see, who have ears but do not hear." (Jer. 5:21)

SIR, WE WISH TO SEE JESUS

To really get Jesus, therefore, meaning to view Him through the lens John intends, I believe we, the readers, must imitate the Greeks who implored Philip, "Sir, we wish to see Jesus." Next, we must clear away any debris that gets in the way. John is like a trainer, signaling commands designed to keep us focused, to stay on point, and not break from it. A.W. Tozer described the process this way:

> The progression will be something like this: First a sound as of a Presence walking in the garden. Then a voice, more intelligible, but still far from clear. Then the happy moment when the Spirit begins to illuminate the Scriptures and that which had been only a sound, or, at best, a voice, now becomes an intelligible word, warm and intimate and clear as the word of a dear friend. Then will come light and life and best of all, ability to see and rest in and embrace Jesus Christ as Savior and Lord of all.[66]

To get started, look at Chapter 9, where a man blind from birth gets healed by Jesus. We'll pick up in verse 11 after he was asked, "How then were your eyes opened?" But there's a catch: we'll put your knowledge to the test with some trivia at the end. Specifically, the man's understanding of who Jesus is evolves the longer the story goes. It's drastic. Jesus' physical opening is obvious, but can you determine how the man's spiritual eyes open? You decide.

> So they were saying to him, "how then were your eyes opened?" 11He answered, "The man who is called Jesus made clay, and anointed my eyes, and said to me, 'Go to Siloam and wash'; so I went away and washed, and I received sight." 12They said to him, "Where is He?" He said, "I do not know."

---

[66] Tozer, A.W., *The Pursuit of God*

13They brought to the Pharisees the man who was formerly blind. 14Now it was a Sabbath on the day when Jesus made the clay and opened his eyes. 15Then the Pharisees also were asking him again how he received his sight. And he said to them, "He applied clay to my eyes, and I washed, and I see." 16Therefore some of the Pharisees were saying, "This man is not from God, because He does not keep the Sabbath." But others were saying, "How can a man who is a sinner perform such signs?" And there was a division among them. 17So they said to the blind man again, "What do you say about Him, since He opened your eyes?" And he said, "He is a prophet."

18The Jews then did not believe it of him, that he had been blind and had received sight, until they called the parents of the very one who had received his sight, 19and questioned them, saying, "Is this your son, who you say was born blind? Then how does he now see?" 20His parents answered them and said, "We know that this is our son, and that he was born blind; 21but how he now sees, we do not know; or who opened his eyes, we do not know. Ask him; he is of age, he will speak for himself." 22His parents said this because they were afraid of the Jews; for the Jews had already agreed that if anyone confessed Him to be Christ, he was to be put out of the synagogue. 23For this reason his parents said, "He is of age; ask him."

24So a second time they called the man who had been blind, and said to him, "Give glory to God; we know that this man is a sinner." 25He then answered, "Whether He is a sinner, I do not know; one thing I do know, that though I was blind, now I see." 26So they said to him, "What did He do to you? How did He open your eyes?" 27He answered them, "I told you already and you did not listen; why do you want to hear it again? You do not want to become His disciples too, do you?" 28They reviled him and said, "You are His disciple, but we are disciples of Moses. 29We know that God has spoken to Moses, but as for this man, we do not know where He is from." 30The man answered and said to them, "Well, here is an amazing thing, that you do not know where He is from, and yet He opened my eyes. 31We know that God does not hear sinners; but if anyone is God-fearing and does His will, He hears him. 32Since the beginning of time it has never been heard that anyone opened the eyes of a person born blind. 33If this man were not from God, He could do nothing." 34They answered him, "You were born entirely in sins, and are you teaching us?" So they put him out.

35Jesus heard that they had put him out, and finding him, He said, "Do you believe in the Son of Man?" 36He answered, "Who is He, Lord, that I may believe in Him?" 37Jesus said to him, "You have both seen Him, and He is the one who is talking with you." 38And he said, "Lord, I believe." And he worshiped Him. (John 9:10-38)

ABILITY TO SEE AND REST AND EMBRACE

verse 11 - The healed man initially views Jesus as a mere_____.

verse 17 – A great leap occurs when he perceives Jesus is a _____.

verses 27-28 – If the healed man claims to be a disciple, by implication Jesus must be his _____.

verse 33 – Jesus, he determines, must be _____.

verse 36 – No longer a mere man, or prophet, but One worthy of the title _____ .

verse 38 – For the first time in history a person acknowledges Jesus is God. How do we know that?[67] Try and determine for yourself before looking at the answer in the footnote.

What's the story underneath the story? A parallel exists; the crowd could see Jesus visually but remained in the dark spiritually. The blind man, on the other hand, saw Jesus in a physical **and** spiritual sense: "Lord, I believe."

On a practical note, and I think this is partly what John was getting at by including chapter 9, I'm persuaded that what transpired in and through the healed man must also occur in us. Depending on the person, we all fall somewhere between being spiritually blind, cloudy, or seeing as bright as the noonday sun. It often takes time to see with eyes to see; it's a process that is typically faster for some and slower for others. On a spiritual spectrum, like the one outlined above from John 9, ask yourself, "Where did I fall 10 years ago? What about 20, or even more recently than that?" If the Lord was patient with you back then, and I'm sure He's patient with you now, how could you not forward that patience to others in return? Jesus never browbeat the blind man for failure to see. Neither should we. Outright sin is one thing, but growing in grace is entirely another. Why would the Lord be longsuffering towards you when you could not see, "such were some of you, but you were washed"[68] and think it's okay to turn around and blast another person for less than 20/20 vision? Always remember that Jesus meets us where we are, no matter where on that spectrum we find ourselves. What's most vital is that we ultimately see and

---

[67] Man / Prophet / Rabbi / from God / Lord / God because "he worshipped Jesus" every Jew knew there was only One true God

[68] *Such were some of you; but you were washed, but you were sanctified, but you were justified in the name of the Lord Jesus Christ and in the Spirit of our God.* – 1st Corinthians 6:11

believe. That's it. And how could you not after reading this Beloved Disciple's Gospel of belief?

Discussion Questions for "John: What Do You Want Us to See?"

Last Week:

The issues of forgiveness and restoration can be painful processes. Did last week's exercise help you take any meaningful steps forward?

Observation and Reflection:

1. What stands out to you the most from the story of the two men in the hospital room and the analogy drawn from it?

2. Reflect on a time when someone's description or encouragement gave you hope or helped you see things differently.

Analogies and Stories:

3. Compare and contrast the two animal stories shared in the chapter. How do they illustrate the theme of missing Jesus or failing to see Him for who He truly is?

4. Reflect on the significance of the blind man's spiritual journey in John 9, considering his progression from viewing Jesus as a mere man to acknowledging Him as Lord and God.

5. How can we extend patience and grace to others who may not yet see Jesus clearly, just as Jesus demonstrated patience towards the blind man?

Further Study:

6. Explore other passages in the Gospel of John where people encounter Jesus but fail to fully understand Him (e.g., Nicodemus in John 3, the Samaritan woman in John 4). What insights can you gain from these encounters? Add them to the chart below.

John 3
John 4
John ___

7. Consider the excerpt of A. W. Tozer's perspective on spiritual progression and the illumination of Scripture. How does his view align with the themes discussed in the chapter?

Response to the Text:

8. How does the chapter challenge you to deepen your belief in Jesus and to see Him more clearly in your life?

9. Share a prayer request based on what you've learned from the chapter and the questions discussed.

Action Steps for Next Week:

In what ways do you relate to the blind man's journey of spiritual sight? How has your understanding of Jesus evolved over time? A healthy exercise would be to divide up your story into 3 to 5 stages and give headers for each stage. Allow participants 15 minutes to unpack their journeys to the rest of the group when you meet. See two examples below:

Tyler:

- Myths and Fables Phase (childhood to 42) – Perceived Bible as fiction at best

- Heart Tugged Phase (43 to 48) – Curiosity piqued; unable to disregard Christianity outright

- Trying to Figure It Out Phase (49 to present)

Sydney:

- Warm and Fuzzy Phase (youth to 15) - Participated in youth activities at church but leaned predominately on parent's faith

- Faith as an Afterthought Phase (16-18)

- Troubled Waters Phase (College years) – Placed Christ on backburner

- Taking Personal Ownership Phase (22-present)

Create your own analogy of what knowing Christ feels like, and how you might express that to a non-believer, similar to the Double Delight rose example. Commit to sharing it with at least one person before you next meet. You can use the following chart or write it out in your own way.

NOUN	DESIRING
WHY	SUMMARY

PART III

What Do You Want Us To Do?

CHAPTER 9

Matthew, What Do You Want Us to do?

"Have New Eyes to See"

WHO IS THE MERCHANT? WHO IS THE PEARL? (99% OF PEOPLE MISS THIS)

At the end of the day, I'm inclined to believe Matthew, at least in part, and not in a self-glorifying sense, wants us to perceive ourselves through the lens by which The Savior beholds us. We are the apple of *His eye*, a fine piece of artwork, a masterpiece, or better yet, a fine jewel. I wonder if that's why he chose to include Matthew 13:45-46.

Christ was fond of speaking in parables, although His listeners often got frustrated, preferring the simple explanation instead, asking, *"Why do You speak in parables?"*

Consider human history and how it cyclically demonstrates man's intense longing for discovery. Hide and seek, for instance, loses all intrigue if the one hiding goes undiscovered. We have an innate sense that anything worth having is worth the time and effort necessary to seek it out. Before reading further, you must stop here and determine for yourself what Jesus was referring to in Matthew 13:45-46;

otherwise, you will miss out on the joy of discovery. As Marcel Proust observed, "*The real voyage of discovery consists not in seeking new landscapes, but in having new eyes.*" So here it is.

> "The kingdom of heaven is like a merchant seeking fine pearls, and upon finding one pearl of great value, he went and sold everything he had and bought it."
>
> – Jesus

The majority of answers go along the following lines, including the overwhelming number of Bible Commentaries:

> It is the person who is the merchant, who at all costs must seek out Christ or seek out the Gospel, in which case He is the finest of pearls, even if it means abandoning everything one has at his or her disposal. After all, who would not gladly forfeit all the riches of this world in exchange for the immeasurable riches of Christ? A refusal to do so would be utterly unwise and foolish.

While some of those sentiments are *partly* true, that's nowhere close to what Christ was referring to. Consider this: what on planet Earth does the natural man or woman possess that could be sold to purchase the invaluable Gospel of Jesus? Next comes the question of who is ultimately seeking out whom. Using the "Parable of the 99," Jesus taught, "For the Son of Man has come to save that which was lost…If a man has a hundred sheep, and one of them has gone astray, does he not leave the ninety-nine on the mountains and go and search for the one that is straying?"[69]

Beyond the shadow of a doubt, Christ Jesus Himself is identified as the Merchant. Before He appeared to us as One of us, hence the Christmas Story, He was the Crown Jewel of the cosmos, with the entirety of the created realm under His dominion. And yet, because of

---

[69] Matthew 18:11-12

the great love with which He loves you, He willingly laid it all aside in exchange for you, His bride. Do you get it? *You, then, are that fine pearl of great value!* You are deemed so priceless (in fact, His followers are "*masterpieces*" in His eyes) He lovingly paid for you as an individual with His very life:

> Although He existed in the form of God, did not regard equality with God a thing to be grasped, but emptied Himself, taking the form of a bond-servant, and being made in the likeness of men. Being found in appearance as a man, He humbled Himself by becoming obedient to the point of death, even death on a cross. (Philippians 2:6-8)

George Eliot observed, "*We are all humiliated by the sudden discovery of a fact which has existed very comfortably and perhaps been staring at us in private while we have been making up our world entirely without it.*" There's no need to be **humiliated** by missing the parable's point if you did. There is, however, a reason to be **humbled** by the parable's point. Its message must transform us. Man is never more driven to labor for the Kingdom of God than when he realizes his worth in it. Good works flow out of our identity in Christ; they don't create it.

May you experience the fullest richness of life by greatly valuing the Merchant while marveling at how greatly He values you. After all, as Oliver Wendell Holmes says, "*A mind stretched by a new experience can never go back to its old dimensions.*"

Discussion Questions for "Matthew, What Do You Want Us to do?"

Last Week:

Share your analogies with the group.

Understanding the Parable

1.   What is the central message of the parable of the merchant seeking fine pearls, as described in Matthew 13:45-46?

2.   How does this parable relate to the kingdom of heaven?

Personal Reflection

3.   Reflect on the idea that Christ, as the Merchant, sought out the fine pearl, which represents you as an individual. How does this perspective change your understanding of your worth and value in God's eyes?

Comparison with Other Parables

4.   Using the provided graph, compare the parable of the merchant seeking fine pearls with other parables spoken by Jesus. How does this parable complement or contrast with other teachings of Jesus?

MERCHANT
TALENTS
FEAST

Application to Life

5. If God sees believers as masterpieces, how does that understanding impact the way you view yourself and your relationship with God?

6. How does it influence your priorities and values in life?

Practical Implications

7. Discuss practical ways in which knowing your value in Christ can influence your daily life, relationships, and decision-making.

Action Step for Next Week:

Each day, write down one way that you either see your value from the lens of God or how knowing your value influenced your actions.

CHAPTER 10

Mark, What Do You Want Us to do?

"Shout Wow"

A few years ago, on CBS Evening News, there was a story about a concert by the Handel and Haydn Society in Boston. The performance featured some of the best classical musicians in the country. However, the most memorable moment of the concert did not come from the performers on stage but from the audience. After the exhilarating crescendo of Mozart's Masonic Funeral Music, someone in the audience shouted, "Wow!" This departure from typical audience protocol and etiquette resonated in the hall and throughout the classical music community. The president of the Society, David Snead, was thrilled by the sense of wonder in the "wow" and determined to find the person who exclaimed it. It turned out to be a 9-year-old boy named Ronan, who was there with his grandfather, Stephen Mattin. Ronan was autistic and considered non-verbal. Until that moment, his family had been told he would never utter a spoken word. However, the beautiful music of the concert awakened a dormant sense of wonder in a word: Wow!

Should Mark's composition, which is far more exhilarating than Mozart's, cease to awaken wonder in our soul, be terribly alarmed. There is nothing more inexcusable than yawning at Handel's "Hallelujah" chorus while remaining comfortably seated on your hands; such nonchalance would rest exclusively on you. Our reaction must impersonate the awestruck Centurion who exclaimed, "Surely this man was the Son of God!"[70] Or, in today's language, "Wow!"

While visiting Old Faithful in Yellowstone National Park, author Philip Yancey made this observation:

> Glancing over my shoulder I saw that not a single waiter or busboy—not even those who had finished their chores—looked out the huge windows. Old Faithful, grown entirely too familiar, had lost its power to impress them. Religious faith can work the same way. Jews in the 19th century France had a saying to describe the decline of spiritual ardor over the generations: "The grandfather prays in Hebrew, the father reads the prayers in French, the son does not pray at all."

Imagine religious faith becoming *entirely too familiar*; just the ring of those three words sounds cold, sterile, and distant. Have you allowed certain content found in Mark to become commonplace? Recall examples such as these. "If You are willing, You can make me clean," begged the leper. "I am willing," Jesus said, "be cleansed." Or what about "Teacher, do You not care that we are perishing?" To which our Lord rebuked the wind and said to the sea, "Hush, be still!" The disciples were astonished and left to ask, "Who then is this, that even the wind and the sea obey Him?" What about you? Are you guilty of domesticating stories like those? Have they, too, lost the power to impress? Again, if yes, I say be greatly alarmed.

---

[70] Mark 15:39

REDOUBLING

In the summer of 1991, after her senior year at Auburn, my wife Jill ventured out on a 1,774-mile trek westward. Her destination was Yellowstone National Park, specifically Canyon Village. Just three years before her arrival, the sites, scenery, and landscape of America's most venerated park had been forever altered. The '88 fires, as they became ominously known, ravaged 36% of the entire park; an astonishing 1.4 million acres went up in flames. Then, on September 11th, 1988, the fires finally subsided thanks to a quarter inch of snowfall.

The mourning process for what Yellowstone "had once been" started soon after that. Many felt that the rare flowers unique to the region would never blossom again—atypical foliage is gone forever. Breeds of wildlife that were nearing extinction edged closer to the brink. Such language makes one wonder: **when did humanity first lose sight of God's neat way of making wrongs just right**?

Have we grown so worldly-wise as to cast off a simple childhood refrain, "He's got the whole world in His hands?" According to Hebrews 13:8, "Jesus Christ is the same yesterday, today, and forever." The world, therefore, remains ever secure in His hands, even in its roughest shape.

RESURGENCE

The Yellowstone recovery from the fires began almost immediately, with plants such as *fireweed* appearing in a matter of days. Wildflowers proliferated beyond everyone's imagination, as if they were clothed more than King Solomon in all his glory. *Aspens*—long a species of concern in the northern Rockies—appeared in areas of the park where, to everyone's knowledge, they had not previously existed. And with one genius stoke from the Vinedresser's hand, seeds that require fire to open, like *lodgepole pines*, could finally germinate. The regeneration in Yellowstone was so vast that no replanting was attempted. Be sure to note that if the Lord can bring light out of said devastation, how much more can God shine glory into whatever desperate situation you're facing?

As for my wife Jill, it had been 34 years and four children later since she last saw Yellowstone. Our family returned there in 2017; it was the best trip of our lifetime. The sites, scenery, and landscape of America's most revered park hadn't lost their luster. No one flower, animal, or foliage had lost its power to impress, unlike the yawns and lackadaisical nature of Old Faithful's employees, to which Yancey referred. Regrowth, recovery, and revitalization all transpired after 1988, sending us away saying, "Oh wow!"

If I were to guess, a number of you are likely surrounded by fires burning beyond your control, most centered around broken relationships. Family tends to be at the top of the list. Nothing speaks to your shambled situation better or instills greater hope to mend it in the future than a verse like Mark 7:37 which says, "They were utterly astonished, saying, 'He has done all things well; He makes even the deaf to hear and the mute to speak.'" **So be encouraged and keep your chin up; the Lord God has a neat way of making many such wrongs just right.**

Discussion Questions for "Mark, What Do You Want Us to do?"

Last Week:

Report your notes from this past week about your value in Christ.

Application of Scripture

1. How does the story of Ronan, the boy who exclaimed "Wow!" at a classical music concert, relate to the concept of maintaining wonderment in our faith?

2. Reflect on instances in your life where religious faith may have become too familiar or commonplace. How can you rekindle a sense of awe and wonder in your spiritual journey?

Comparison to Yellowstone Park

3. What parallels can you draw between the devastation and regeneration of Yellowstone Park after the 1988 fires and the potential for spiritual renewal in our lives?

4. Discuss Hebrews 13:8 ("Jesus Christ is the same yesterday and today, and forever") in the context of enduring faith amid life's challenges and changes.

Personal Reflection

5. Have you ever experienced a moment where your faith was revitalized or renewed? Describe that experience and its impact on your spiritual journey.

6. Consider broken relationships or challenges in your life. How can the examples of resilience and renewal discussed in this chapter inspire hope and perseverance in your situation?

Group Discussion

7. Share instances where you have witnessed or experienced the power of God's renewal or restoration in your life or the lives of others.

8. How can we encourage one another to maintain a sense of wonder and awe in our faith journey, even amidst familiarity or challenges?

Action Step for Next Week:

Think of a broken relationship in your life burning beyond your control. Is there an olive branch you can extend as a first step towards reconciliation? If yes, what might that look like? If now is not the time to make such a move, do not feel guilty. The Lord appoints a perfect time for every matter under heaven. But at the very least, pray about being receptive to this notion one day in the future.

CHAPTER 11

Luke, What Do You Want Us to do?

"Get It Right This Time"

A young couple moved to a new neighborhood. The next morning, the young woman saw her neighbor hanging the wash outside while they were having breakfast. She commented that the laundry wasn't clean and suggested that her neighbor might need better laundry soap. Her husband remained quiet. Every time the neighbor would hang her wash, the young woman would make similar comments. After a month, the young woman noticed that the neighbor's laundry was clean and wondered who taught her. Her husband explained that he had cleaned their windows that morning, and this allowed them to see things more clearly. And so it is with life. What we see when watching others depends on the purity of the window through which we look. "Why do you look at the speck that is in your brother's eye, but do not notice the log that is in your own eye?" (Luke 6:41)

It's implausible, or at least it should be, to identify the hypocrisy of others in a book like Luke while neglecting to see it in ourselves, hence the log and speck analogy. The temptation to do so is unavoidable; the willingness to fight against it is not.

In ancient times, actors used to wear different masks to play various roles, and this practice led to the term "two-faced" in modern English.

In the New Testament, written in Greek, actors were referred to as *hypokrités,* which translates to "hypocrite" in English. I find Philip Yancey's observation on this concept fascinating.

> Having spent time around "sinners" and also around purported saints, I have a hunch why Jesus spent so much time with the former group: I think He preferred their company. Because the sinners were honest about themselves and had no pretense, Jesus could deal with them. In contrast, the saints put on airs, judged Him, and sought to catch Him in a moral trap. In the end it was the saints, not the sinners, who arrested Jesus.[71]

The feeling of dissonance between one's actions and beliefs is not unique to Christianity, but has persisted throughout history. Even the military conqueror, Alexander the Great, who was known for his ruthless tactics and pagan religion, recognized this disparity. When a deserter was brought before him, the automatic sentence for any deserter in battle was immediate death. However, moments before the execution was to occur, Alexander the Great asked the man his name. The man replied that his name was Alexander. Upon hearing this, Alexander the Great stated that the man would be pardoned under one condition: either he should change his ways or change his name.

What's so difficult to understand about Luke 6:46, "Now why do you call Me, 'Lord, Lord,' and do not do what I say?" Or, how about, "The one who has heard and has not acted accordingly is like a man who built a house on the ground without a foundation; and the river burst against it and it immediately collapsed, and the ruin of that house was great" (Luke 6:49). Or lastly, "There is nothing covered up that will not be revealed, and nothing hidden that will not be known. Accordingly, whatever you have said in the dark will be heard in the light, and what

---

[71] Yancey, Philip. *What's So Amazing About Grace?*

you have whispered in the inner rooms will be proclaimed upon the housetops" (Luke 12:2–3).

THE WORLD DOESN'T READ THE BIBLE; THE WORLD READS CHRISTIANS

So, let's get it right this time. Our past hypocrisy is inexcusable. 2000 years' worth of mixed messaging is plenty enough to last an eternity. We've left countless lost souls in our wake, but no longer will we continue handing out excuses for the denial of the Gospel's message. Instead, we invite others to do as we do, not only as we say. Quite simply, we're putting our money where our mouth is through a simple challenge borrowed from the Apostle Paul, who stated, "Imitate me as I imitate Christ" (1 Corinthians 11:1). It's that simple. From now on, we will be known by the fruit that we produce: love, joy, kindness, gentleness, faithfulness, goodness, patience, and self-control (Galatians 5:22-23), and nothing less.

The best example to set comes from Dr. W.H. Houghton, who pastored the Calvary Baptist Church in NYC and later served as president of Moody Bible Institute. When Dr. Houghton became pastor of the Baptist Tabernacle in Atlanta, a man in that city hired a private detective to follow Dr. Houghton and report on his conduct. After a few weeks, the detective could report to the man that Dr. Houghton's life matched his preaching. As a result of Houghton's faithful life, a life of integrity, that man became a Christian. May we do no less. "*The eye is the lamp of your body; when your eye is clear, your whole body also is full of light; but when it is bad, your body also is full of darkness. Then watch out that the light in you is not darkness. If therefore your whole body is full of light, with no dark part in it, it will be wholly illumined, as when the lamp illumines you with its rays*" (Luke 11:34-36).

Discussion Questions for "Luke, What Do You Want Us to do?"

Last Week:

Did you have an occasion to extend an olive branch to someone you've been at odds with? How did it go? Reconciliation is a multi-step process that takes time. It can be painful, as well as agonizing. A first-step might not solve years of pent-up issues, but it can be a start. Stop here for a few moments as a group to pray for members struggling through this. A solution might not exist, but to hear friends who care praying for you goes a long way.

The Laundry Analogy

1. How does the story of the young couple and their neighbor's laundry illustrate the concept of seeing others through a clear window?

2. What does Luke 6:41 teach us about the tendency to notice flaws in others while overlooking our own?

Alexander the Great Story

3. What lessons can we learn from the story of Alexander the Great and the deserter?

4. How does this story emphasize the importance of aligning actions with beliefs?

Living Out Our Faith

5. What messages do Luke 6:46, Luke 6:47-49, Luke 12:2-3, and Luke 11:34-36 convey about authenticity and integrity in faith?

6. In what ways can Christians better reflect the teachings of Jesus in their daily lives, as suggested in the passage?

Impact of Integrity

7. What role does integrity play in influencing others and sharing the message of Christianity?

Interpretation of Luke 11:34-36

8. What does Luke 11:34-36 mean by having a "clear eye," and how does it relate to living a life of integrity?

Action Step for Next Week:

Get uncomfortable. Using the graph below, write down every time you point out someone else's flaw and every time you acknowledge your own. Which column is bigger?

SPECK	LOG

CHAPTER 12

John, What Do You Want Us to do?

"Don't Walk By as if Nothing"

"Is it nothing to you, all who pass by?" -
Lamentations 1:12

This is the true story of a Missouri man named John Griffith, who worked as a drawbridge controller on the Mississippi River. I trust that what he did, like what God the Father and God the Son did on Good Friday in 30 AD, will stop you dead in your tracks.

One day, in the summer of 1937, John Griffith decided to take his eight-year-old son, Greg, with him to work. At noon, he put the bridge up to allow ships to pass and sat on the observation deck with his son to eat lunch. The time passed quickly. Suddenly, he was startled by the shrieking of a train whistle in the distance. He quickly looked at his watch and noticed it was 1:07. The Memphis Express had four hundred passengers on board, and it was roaring toward the raised bridge!

John leaped from the observation deck and ran back to the control tower. Just before throwing the master lever, he glanced down for any ships below. There was a sight that caught his eye causing his heart to leap to his throat. His eight-year-old son, Greg, had slipped from the observation deck and had fallen into the massive gears that operated the bridge. His leg was caught in the cogs of two main gears! Desperately, John's mind whirled to devise a rescue plan. But as soon as he thought of a possibility, he knew there was no way he could do it. Again, with alarming closeness, the train whistle shrieked. He could hear the clicking of the locomotive wheels over the tracks. That was his son down there, yet there were four hundred passengers on the train. John knew what he had to do, so he buried his head in his left arm and pushed the master switch forward. That great, massive bridge was lowered into place just as the Memphis Express began to roar across the river.

When John Griffith lifted his head, he looked into the passing windows of the train. There were businessmen casually reading their afternoon papers, finely dressed ladies in the dining car sipping coffee, and children pushing long spoons into their dishes of ice cream. No one looked at the control house, and no one looked at the great gearbox. With wrenching agony, John Griffith cried out at the steel train, "I sacrificed my son for you, people! Don't you care?" The train rushed by, but nobody heard the father's words.

The Prophet Jeremiah asks, *"Is it nothing to you, all who pass by?"* (Lamentations 1:12)

I suppose all of us have been, even for extended periods of time, no different than those passengers of the Memphis Express: casually going about our own daily business, or perhaps too stressed out from the craziness of life to take notice of something like a mere cross.

Crosses now adorn all of society—too much, I believe. They have become fashionable for the religious and irreligious alike, with no discernible divide between the secular and sacred. They're imprinted on your t-shirts, nonchalantly so. They currently hang as decorative pieces accenting the décor in your living room. I've never cared to see their presence in bathrooms. Please don't do that. Your person likely exhibits one at present; what once evoked horror and extreme sorrow hardly now gleans a second glance.

In summary, we've grown all too familiar with the ever-presence of crosses; the inherent shock value they once possessed has by and large dissipated over time. As a test, if I told you that you're familiar with the word Israelites use for whole burnt offerings, I might solicit a yawn. But if I go on to explain that the Hebrew word is *Holocaust*, well, your attention gets caught. What Christ underwent at Calvary was, in every sense, a *holocaust*. Consider using holocaust in place of the cross from time to time to retain the horror contained therein.

If, only for a while, you were to stop dead in your tracks at the sight of a cross, my purpose in writing the *4 Faces of Christ* would be made complete. Otherwise, my efforts are in vain. **To pose the question from Jeremiah once again: *"Is it nothing to you, all who pass by?"*** I trust the answer will be no...at least for now.

Discussion Questions for "John, What Do You Want Us to do?"

Last Week:

Share with your group which column was larger. Discuss why you personally struggle with clear eyes in your own life.

Impact of Indifference

1. How does the indifference of the Memphis Express passengers parallel with how people often respond to Jesus' sacrifice?

Familiarity with the Cross

2. Discuss the author's observations about the familiarity of crosses in society today.

3. Do you agree that the shock value of the cross has diminished over time? Why or why not?

Holocaust vs. Cross

4. What significance does the author attach to using the word "holocaust" instead of "cross"?

5. How might this shift in language affect our perception of Christ's sacrifice?

Personal Response:

6. Are there areas in your life where you've grown indifferent or complacent about the significance of Jesus' sacrifice?

Application in Daily Life:

7. What practical steps can you take to keep the message of the cross fresh and impactful in your heart and mind?

Scripture Connection:

8. How does Jeremiah's question, "Is it nothing to you, all who pass by?" (Lamentations 1:12), resonate with the message of the chapter?

9. What might the artwork depicting crosses in your home or on your person say about your attitude towards the crucifixion?

10. Close your time with prayer asking God to make the horror of the cross more evident every day, or confession for taking Christ's sacrifice lightly if you have.

EPILOGUE

Now, as we stand at the culmination of the Four Faces of Christ and glance back across the various depictions of our Savior—from the Lamb, gentle and bearing our sins, to the Lion, triumphant and roaring through eternity, from the Servant who washed filthy feet to the Word that spoke all of creation into being—if I were to inquire, similar to my mother who echoed softly in her beautiful, long-winded southern drawl—"Now then, what do you see?" any response even closely resembling "More of Him and less of me," would make my joy in writing this complete.

Add to that meaningful dialogue, I trust, spurred on by the discussion questions among your group, along with weekly tasks to increase your participation in the Gospel work at hand; well, such immense satisfaction comes with that.

But don't stop here. Let me invite you to keep digging deeper into the heart of Scripture because a new gem of gospel truth emerges to the fore when you think you've read it all a million times before. It's not dissimilar to fine particles of gold waiting to be found. As the introduction states, "There's always more to see...but you must look for it." I can certainly promise you that.